Every  person is assigned a mission by God. In fact, ever since God created the universe, He arranged the first causes in such a way that the unbroken chain of their effects should create the most favorable conditions and circumstances for each person to fulfill the mission that God has assigned to him.

Therefore, every person is born with abilities that are proportionate to the mission he or she has been entrusted, and throughout each persons whole life, the environment, circumstances and everything else will contribute to make it easy and possible for him or her to reach that purpose.

In fact, each person's perfection consists in reaching that purpose; and the more thoroughly one's mission is fulfilled, the greater and holier he or she shall be before the eyes of God.

Besides natural gifts, every person is also accompanied by the grace of God from the cradle to the tomb. God's grace is poured on each one of us in such quantity and quality that our weak human nature strengthens itself by acquiring the supernatural energy we need to face our own mission.

<u>**Saint Maximilian Kolbe**</u>

If You Wish To Be Perfect

(Matthew 19:21)

Including:

A Simple Conversion Guide For Catholics

by: Joe Stevens

1663 LIBERTY DRIVE, SUITE 200
BLOOMINGTON, INDIANA 47403
(800) 839-8640
WWW.AUTHORHOUSE.COM

© 2005 Joe Stevens. All Rights Reserved.

No part of this book may be reproduced, stored in a retrieval system, or transmitted by any means without the written permission of the author.

First published by AuthorHouse 08/01/05

ISBN: 1-4208-4801-1 (sc)

Printed in the United States of America
Bloomington, Indiana

This book is printed on acid-free paper.

Table of Contents

Dedication vii
Preface ix

Part 1: His Plan -- My Conversion 1
    Is That All There Is? 3
    Valerie 8
    Searching 14
    Moving On 19
    Treading Water 22
    Vista 27
    The Holy Spirit Speaks 35
    Byways to Heaven 38
    One Bread, One Body 41
    Little Rock Scripture Study 43
    Phoebe 48
    The Year of the Holy Spirit 54
    What Do We Do With the Truth? 68
    SPAN 74
    The Year of God the Father 77
    Jubilee 83
    What Now, Lord? 91
    Year of the Not So Holy Family 98
    Is That All There Is??? 100

Part 2: A Simple Conversion Guide for Catholics ... 103
    Introduction 105
    Step 1 – Believe 109

Step 2 – Pray 112
Step 3 – Listen 125
Step 4 – God's Plan 150
Step 5 – Gifts 156
Step 6 – Lifestyle 171
Step 7 – Love 195
Step 8 – The Cross 201
Step 9 – Conversion Revisited 207
Appendix 210

Dedication

Dedicated to:

The Holy Spirit

Valerie – wife and partner

Father Al Lauer
(1947 – 2002)

The trinity of my conversion.

Preface

Many remember the parable of **The Rich Young Man** (Matthew 19:16-22), who asks Jesus, *"What good must I do to gain eternal life?"* Most of us can readily recall the response from our Lord, *"Go sell what you have and give it to the poor, and you will have treasure in Heaven."* That command brings concern to many, who like the rich young man, cannot part with all our possessions. Does that weakness, that inability to share our goods with the poor mean that we cannot go to Heaven? I don't think so.

Let's go back and look at what Jesus really says, as reported by Matthew. He begins with, "If you wish to be perfect." Yes, we are called and gifted by God to become perfect – even Jesus!!! In **"The Letter to the Hebrews,"** chapter 5, we read, *"Son though he was, he learned obedience from what he suffered; and when he was made perfect, he became the source of eternal salvation for all who obey him."* We are called to try to become perfect. For most, it doesn't mean that we must become poor to be saved. So what does it mean? That, my friend, is the message of this book.

In Part 1 I share the ongoing story of my conversion to someone trying to understand and live my calling. In my case, the Holy Spirit chose to provide a personal trainer we call "Phoebe." Part 2 is an effort to help others, like yourself, to hear and respond to God's individual call and revelation of your precise role in His Salvation Plan. Yes, God calls each and every one of us to the perfection of a predetermined position. In this world that He created, all animals, insects, plants, climate, etc. contribute to the balance of nature. We human beings are created to contribute our specialties to the balance of God's Kingdom on earth so that we may come to share the eternal life He promised.

Do we need to reach perfection before we enter the Kingdom of Heaven? I hope not, or most of us will live longer than Methuselah. For most, like myself, conversion, or the journey to perfection doesn't start until our later years. It was my 58th year before I even began to recognize the need for a stronger relationship with the Father, Son, and Holy Spirit. This should have been a surprise, considering my status as a "cradle Catholic." Actually being born in the faith may have slowed my recognizing a need for conversion, but thanks to God and Phoebe, the journey began, and so can yours. It's amazing as we progress how many other truth seekers we meet along *the way*.

About three years ago I started to encounter the many conversion stories of Catholics like Scott Hahn, Jeff Cavin, Marcus Grodi, and numerous others. There is even a weekly TV series on the Eternal Word Television Network (Mother Angelica's Catholic channel) called "The Journey Home." Each week a different guest shares the story of their return to Catholicism. Most conversions are from other religions that occurred from a new or more intense study of Scripture. It came to mind that God might be calling me to share my story. You begin to think this way after opening your heart to the Holy Spirit. And why not? My conversion stems from a new and more intense exposure to Scripture. Although I was never a minister like many of those on the show, my tale is every bit as true and dramatic. It may even be more meaningful since it is not even from another religion. My conversion was from a cradle Catholic mentality to disciple in training. It also includes the conversion from alcoholic to over 13 years of sobriety, from Bible illiterate to Bible Study teacher and many, many changes in lifestyle, but that's getting ahead of the story. In case you're wondering, Phoebe doesn't enter the scene for quite a while, but be patient – she is well worth waiting for.

If You Wish To Be Perfect

(Matthew 19:21)

Part 1:

His Plan -- My Conversion

Is That All There Is?

Where do I start? You certainly don't need to know about my entire 67 years. There are, however, a few early details that are important.

While growing up in Baltimore, my family followed all the rules. I think most everyone did in those "Happy Days". We didn't know how poor we were, for the media had not yet begun to tell us. As a family we went to Mass every Sunday and Holy Day. If Mass lasted more than 45 minutes, we became uncomfortable. Of course, we made our Easter duty every year. We would strictly observe the rather stringent Lenten regulations of the times, although I recall at noon on Holy Saturday (the end of Lent), the dining room table was laden with all the traditional Polish Easter dishes. Mom, dad, my two older sisters and I were seated around with forks and knives in hand, having already said grace, waiting for the last toll of the clock, announcing the end of fasting. Looking back at that annual ritual, it now appears somewhat sacrilegious.

Is That All There Is?

There was one exception to my minimalist approach to Catholicism practiced in my earlier years. In 1954 the rest of my family moved to California and I remained in Baltimore to finish high school. For some reason, I started to attend daily Mass on my way to public school. I'm not sure why, and it really didn't help. I ended up flunking my last semester and finishing high school in California. That was my only burst of daily devotion for the next 40 years.

The next phase of my life was probably ideal by many standards. I still feel that the '50s were maybe the last great time to be growing up. After high school I got a job, bought a convertible, started junior college and met the girl of my dreams, I thought. We were both 21 when we married. It never occurred to me that we knew absolutely nothing about each other.

Over the next 10 years we experienced three of God's greatest blessings: Teresa, Julie and Mark. My career in aerospace sales was beginning to take off and so was my drinking. We continued the "Sunday go to Mass" form of our religion. The exception to mediocrity in my faith was when I became one of the first lectors for our church. Although I did not recognize it as such, this was my initial encounter with Scripture.

The day of my first reading, I was a nervous wreck. As requested by me, Sandy and the kids were seated near the back of the church, where I could not see them. The Sunday Scripture was from the book of Genesis, chapter 3, including verse 13. I had gone over it several times looking for difficult names or words, not paying attention to the content. Unfortunately, I read the Bible this way for many years. So I proceeded with the story of Adam and Eve: *"the Lord God then asked the woman, why did you eat the apple?* Just for a brief moment, I wanted to say, in my best Flip Wilson voice, "The devil made me do it", but I didn't. After the Mass, my wife advised, she knew what I wanted to say and was prepared to make a quick exit with the children. Lectoring is still one of my favorite ministries. But now I recognize the honor of being allowed to proclaim The Word of God. The Holy Spirit continues to watch over my reading so the parishioners will hear what God wants them to hear and understand.

Even though we had a nice home, three healthy children and enough money for a few luxuries, my mind began to wonder, "Is That All There Is?" I believe this started prior to Peggy Lee making the phrase popular in song.

After 18 years of going to college whenever I could squeeze in a class, I received a Bachelor of Science degree in Marketing. It was quite exciting to be the first in my family to have that blessing. Unfortunately, both my parents had died when I was in my 20s and didn't get to share my joy. My wife didn't share the moment either.

It was about that time that Sandy informed me that she no longer wanted to be married. Even though we had had some rough times like most young couples, nothing prepared me or the children for that devastating revelation. Though not a devout Catholic, I did believe that marriage was forever, till death do us part. I now realize that we had let the devil into our lives – me with my drinking and she with a newfound interest in the occult.

For me, the alcohol was part of my career in sales. At the time, three-martini lunches were common place. One of my managers, commenting on my drinking, said, "Let me know your brand, so I can send a case to all my other salesmen." I believe that had been said about General Grant during the Civil War. I was a functioning alcoholic but didn't know it. In spite of consuming about half a quart of vodka each day, I never got drunk nor had a serious hangover. I believe it was St. Augustine who wrote that God allowed us to enjoy our sinful addictions, making our repentance more difficult and meaningful. It wasn't until my hands began to shake as I lifted the first drink of the day that the problem became obvious. I solved that by having the first drink in private. However, drinking large quantities and falling asleep at 8:00 each night does not make for a promising marriage. The biggest problem with drinking, at any level, is that it clouds your mind and soul so that God can't enter your heart. This is what makes the first three steps of Alcoholics Anonymous so difficult for most. I'll give my secret for success later.

My wife's involvement with the occult was equally as damaging and hidden from the two of us. The Bible clearly addresses the subject in several places, including Deuteronomy, chapter 19, verses 10 through 14. Verse 12 says, *"anyone who does such things is an abomination to the Lord."*

And so, after 15 years, the marriage ended in divorce and subsequent annulment. The next 13 years for me consisted of being a devoted absentee father, an alcoholic and a fairly decent salesman. And that's all there was.

Before I really got to know God, the one thing that kept my faith going was the deep belief that in this life on earth, regardless of how much success, money, possessions, sex we have, there must be something more, and there is. Otherwise, it just doesn't make any sense at all. When I look back on those years, I have wondered if it was not a waste of precious God-given time. Maybe, but at least I was there for our children. No one or nothing, except alcohol, interfered with that. I can report that they are all three good, Christian, moral adults, contributing to society, not taking away.

Valerie

In future chapters, I will discuss more about God's plan, but for now I would like to share one significant example of how God has that plan for each one of us. My commitment to Teresa, Julie and Mark was paramount in my life. I had made a promise to myself that nothing would come between us as long as they needed me, or to look at it another way, at least until they became adults. In 1987, when my youngest reached 18, God began to reveal my future.

On March 27, 1987 I attended the wedding of my friend Art. At the evening reception a couple of hundred people were seated in groups of eight to 10. Next to me at our table arranged for singles was the most beautiful and radiant woman I had ever met. Apparently my matchmaker friend Art had put her there to meet someone other than myself. This made sense, since Art knew I was bringing a date. It didn't matter – it was already too late, or more likely, just in time. I never believed much in love at first sight, especially at the age of 50, but there it was – bells, whistles and shooting stars surrounded Valerie and me. God wanted to make sure we got the message. On the dance floor, the first statement out of my mouth was, "I'm going to get to know you real well." To my surprise, she replied, "I hope so." And we never looked back. We spent the next two years getting to know each other and having more fun than most people share in a lifetime.

Valerie's husband had died of lung cancer a few years before. If I hadn't recently quit smoking, this relationship would never have materialized – more of God's plan. She had three children about the same age as mine. My children loved her, and hers tolerated me. After 13 years of living alone, I was not much interested in becoming part of a family.

The number of things we had in common would fill this book. Just to mention a few of the important items: First and foremost, our religion; I think we both knew we could never develop a relationship with a non-Catholic. Then there was the age and number of our children and the proximity of our homes – alcoholics prefer not to drive very far. Although we both loved our children, we were now both ready for the next phase in our lives.

We probably would have married immediately except for a couple of giant hurdles. Valerie's daughter was married, but there were two sons living at home. For me, not wanting to take on a family was second only to my primary obstacle: Catholics who divorced are not entitled to remarry until after an annulment. This one item permeated my thoughts for the next two years.

In the spring of 1988 I had a single bypass surgery. The procedure was successful, and six weeks of recuperation provided time to reflect on our relationship. It was during this time that I wrote Valerie a 10-page dissertation on "everything you need to know about Joe but are afraid to ask." It covered what I considered all the major topics that should be paramount to our future, including:

> <u>Love</u> – emotional and physical. I did not yet understand the concept of unconditional love. There was also the very serious issue of sexual relations and our religious beliefs.
>
> <u>Health</u> – The recent surgery had left me feeling vulnerable. Valerie, on the other hand, came from a family blessed, I guess, with longevity.
>
> <u>Drinking</u> – I was not yet willing to admit to alcoholism or think about changing. Fool that she was, Valerie was willing to accept me as is. It caused us both several years of grief.
>
> <u>Family</u> – 13 years of living alone had made me selfish with my time. I was not ready to work on a relationship with her children, and actually, neither were they. And then there were her parents, in their 70s at the time we met.

What would be expected as they grew older and less independent? For me, the idea of someone having to live with us was totally unacceptable. This is a topic we confronted periodically.

<u>Friends</u> – At the time, Valerie had a close circle of friends, many dating back to grammar school. Very nice people who, in my opinion, "didn't drink enough."

<u>Work and Security</u> – This was a period of relative success in my career, but I was still concerned about my financial future. My father had worked at the same job for 20 years and worried about being laid off every day of his life.

<u>Religion</u> – Our mutual Catholicism was a definite plus, and subsequently our faith got us through the rough spots. Our lifestyles, however, were not consistent with our beliefs. We missed a great opportunity to witness to our children and others about abstinence and also divorce.

All things considered, I was not ready for a marriage commitment. I have spent a lot of time on this subject in hopes of being of help to others contemplating matrimony. My approach of putting your feelings into writing was subsequently turned into a magazine article. Valerie chose not to elaborate in writing, but my dissertation did open a floodgate of discussions. So together we continued our journey down the bumpy road of love.

While on vacation in our favorite beach town of Carpinteria, we attended Mass at St. Joseph's Church. The pastor gave his annual fire-and-brimstone homily on the sins of divorce and remarriage. When we returned to our hotel, I informed Valerie of my belief in everything the priest had said and I felt we could not marry. It was truly one of the most difficult decisions I had ever made. We separated for several months. During that time I was miserable and cried a great deal. So I anesthetized my feelings with alcohol but did not get over the sorrow.

I attended another Mass at St. Joseph's, hoping that God would give me a different message through another priest. Catholics have been known to take this approach to problem solving, even though, in the end, it's between us and God. The theme of this homily was "The only sin is not to love." I contemplated and prayed on that for several weeks and made an appointment to speak with the latter priest. During an hour of counseling, he basically encouraged me to follow my heart and give up the things of a child. He then heard my confession and gave me absolution. I asked if he would marry us in the church. He declined. At that point I felt both encouraged and abandoned.

On Christmas Eve 1988, I asked Valerie to marry me. She said yes. We consulted with several priests, but all refused our request for marriage in the Catholic church. On April 1, 1989 we made our vows in a non-denominational ceremony. Let me explain about April 1, lest you think that we did not take our commitment seriously. Valerie, being a sentimental type, wanted to get married on the anniversary of the day we met. In 1989 that turned out to be Holy Saturday, and so we moved it out one week to April Fools Day. We get happy anniversary calls from men who can't remember their own wedding date.

Although I still had misgivings about our non-denominational marriage, annulment was not a consideration. It seemed to me that the church had given way to pressure from wealthy and influential Catholics. Apparently there was no St. Thomas Moore around to fight the battle. However, when I received notice that Sandy had initiated the process to have our marriage annulled, I was elated. The diocese office included several articles explaining the reasons and justification for annulment in some cases. It became clear that even after 15 years of marriage, our union in the Catholic church could rightfully be declared null, and so it was. Valerie and I were married sacramentally, by a Catholic priest at the altar of our Lord and Savior, Jesus Christ. We are doubly blessed with two anniversaries to celebrate. Valerie's love and prayers, I'm convinced, were the beginning of my conversion.

Searching

The first few years of our marriage would have to be called unusual by most standards. Our great love maintained us through some very serious difficulties. For starters, because of my inability to adjust to family living, we kept two houses, one for the benefit of her two sons still living at home. The homes were only three miles apart, and so we bounced from one to the other. It was an odd and frivolous way of living, but completely acceptable to newlyweds. The proximity of the homes was a blessing until the 1993 Northridge earthquake, but more on that later. It wasn't until both Greg and Doug moved out that we were able to settle into our one home.

About six months after we were married, Valerie was diagnosed with breast cancer. It was devastating for her, but hiding in a bottle, I did not recognize the seriousness of the illness until many years later. Looking back, I was of little or no help to Valerie during this crisis. She suffered through a lumpectomy, radiation and brutal chemotherapy, pretty much on her own. God sometimes allows bad things to happen to good people for the blessings that He has in mind. Somewhere in Scripture it says that all gifts are given for the benefit of others. Cancer may be considered a gift of God's own cross, since He also provides the grace to carry it. Fifteen years later, Valerie is cancer free and has started a Christian cancer support group for women in treatment.

After her healing we began to enjoy our newlywed status again, although physically Valerie was never the same. Those of you who have been through the treatment understand the long-term effects – the energy doesn't fully return. It slowed her down just enough so that I was able to keep up. Maybe that was also part of God's plan. We began to grow together, I thought.

A few years into our marriage, my doctor informed me that the drinking was beginning to have an effect on my heart that eventually would cause permanent damage. About the same time, Valerie admitted she probably couldn't spend the rest of her life with an alcoholic. God again realized that I required at least two reasons to quit drinking. The latter, however, surprised me, since she knew of my problem from the start. I thought her to be unfair. Although I was weak, our love and God's love were very strong as we began to pray for my sobriety. Valerie, I'm sure, had been praying for some time.

Although I didn't realize it at the time, the Holy Spirit stepped in. As I drove from customer to customer listening to a local news station, I was suddenly bombarded with commercials for alcoholism treatment centers. After I successfully quit drinking, although still listening to the same radio station, the commercials were never heard from again.

At about 10:00 p.m. on October 21, 1991 I poured half a liter of Wolfschmidt vodka down the kitchen drain while Valerie photographed the event. The next morning she drove me to St. John's Medical Center in Santa Monica for the start of a 30-day program. Thus began the second step of my conversion.

The treatment was based on the first three steps of Alcoholics Anonymous:

> 1. Admitting we were powerless over alcohol and our lives had become unmanageable.
>
> 2. Believing that a power greater than ourselves could restore us to sanity.
>
> 3. Making a decision to turn our lives over to God.

I don't recall committing to any of these ideas, nor was I aware of a 12-step program. Truth be known, when I entered the Chemical Dependence Center, although I knew I was an alcoholic, it didn't seem to make me powerless. I was a functioning alcoholic to most people, including my co-workers. The only ones really aware of my problem were Valerie and our children. Regardless of my feelings, God responded to someone's prayers and took away my addiction on that first day, and I never had to look back.

During the first two days of detox, I was bored from sitting in my room and anxious to get into meetings with the others. There were no physical effects from being without alcohol, even though I had been a daily drinker. Finally on the third morning they introduced me to the other 11 people. Together we were going to share our deepest, darkest secrets, except I didn't really have any. For some of the group I was a serious irritation, and for the rest they probably did not believe I was one of them. All were struggling for sobriety, some were still shaking, and many were having trouble concentrating. One member was so upset that he threatened to throw me out of a third-story window. Thank God he had several days of sobriety behind him.

Like Valerie's cancer, alcoholism was probably another gift from God, for the benefit of others. I didn't even realize that I was being used to evangelize. During treatment, and continuing to this day, I have shared the story of God's healing grace. At least one member of the St. John's Twelve (my recovery group) returned to the Catholic faith. He had been my roommate.

Before I received my 90-day chip, the counselors informed me there was no need for me to continue in the aftercare program. Apparently they were not equipped to handle someone who had been healed so completely. It was disrupting to their routine. To the best of my knowledge, only one or two others from the St. John's Twelve has maintained their sobriety; one is my recovering Catholic roommate.

Infrequently I attend an Alcoholics Anonymous meeting, either to support a struggling friend or to pick up my annual chip. Each time I share my story. Invariably someone approaches me after the meeting to share that they too were healed by God, in the same manner. I tell everyone that my recovery is not the norm and that most need AA meetings for the rest of their lives. Also, I am still an alcoholic. If I had one small glass of wine today, I would be consuming a half liter of vodka tomorrow. That knowledge and the grace of God keeps me sober. There are numerous benefits of sobriety, but none express it better than what was said by my daughter, Julie – "I have my father back." I didn't even know I was gone.

My favorite prayer, which you will encounter several times is:

> Open my heart, Holy Spirit, to receive your word,
> enlighten my mind to understand.
> Strengthen me, Holy Spirit,
> to follow wherever you lead.

At this time my heart was beginning to open. It would be years before I began to understand.

Moving On

Most 12-step programs encourage a significant lifestyle change. No longer should you associate with the same friends or visit the same haunts. Very few in recovery have the luxury of my kind of change. In January 1992 I turned 55 and completed 10 years of employment with Scientific Atlanta. That was the criteria for early retirement, and so I took it. About six months earlier we had purchased a used, 19-foot motor home, and here was the opportunity to use it. In mid January we said goodbye to family and friends and began an eight-and-a-half-month, 26,000-mile journey. Actually, it was more like three journeys.

Mid January through mid February was our shakedown trip, which included Arizona and New Mexico. This is some of the best country for a pilgrimage to old missions and chapels. Later when we showed pictures to our children, their unanimous comments were, "Did you see anything besides churches?" The visits to holy places probably contributed more to my conversion than I realized; for me it was going to be just a really long vacation.

This is a good place to share one of the best-kept secrets of the Catholic faith. It was first told to me in about the 5th grade while at Sacred Heart of Mary Elementary School in Baltimore. I remember one of the teaching nuns saying, "Every time you go to Mass and receive the Eucharist at a church you had not previously visited and say three each of Our Father, Hail Mary and Glory Be, you get to make a wish and <u>God must grant you that wish</u>." Sound too good to be true? Just try it. We celebrated Mass at many new churches and made a lot of wishes. All of them have been granted, by the grace of God, and believe me, some of them were very heavy duty, approaching miracle status. When I don't have anything important to wish for, I say the prayers and ask God to give my wish to someone who really needs one at that moment. No, I can't tell you what my wishes were – that's part of the mystique.

Even at the beginning stage of my spiritual journey, I had two major benefits going for me: I am Polish, and I am childlike in my faith, believing everything the church teaches. This has now been expanded to include every word of the Bible. Jesus didn't say we had to be Polish, but He did say we must become like little children.

Well, back to the travels. The next two legs of our trip were about three months each. The first was from Los Angeles to the eastern coast of Florida and back.

After a brief family visit, we traveled to Maine and back. Except for weekly Mass and occasional visits to some of the major Catholic shrines and cathedrals, there wasn't anything exceptionally religious about the whole vacation. After we were home for several months, we began discussing our next trip.

Although sharing eight and one half months of close living and new adventures was very exciting, we both agreed that there had been something missing. Most people we talk to, including one priest, admit a little envy at our experience. That's when I quote from Tony Campolo's book "Wake Up America": "Life is meant to be more than traveling around in recreational vehicles, towing boats."

Treading Water

The two years following our marathon trip were uneventful from a religious standpoint. We both knew that God had something in store for us, but we probably were not ready. Valerie did join a women's prayer group, and I volunteered as an alternate usher during the holidays. That was about all I could muster. Oh yes, a friend invited me to a couple of the major Promise Keeper weekends. It introduced me to a new kind of charismatic Christianity I had never experienced. Years later it would prove to be a significant stepping stone on my spiritual journey.

Our family was beginning to grow. During the first 10 years together, we averaged a new grandchild every year. Valerie's daughter Debbie and husband Bill had moved to Las Vegas, while the rest of the family remained in Southern California. Valerie was thoroughly enjoying the grandma role, which was a side of her I wasn't prepared for. Also, I wasn't ready for all this family togetherness. Years of drinking and living alone had taken its toll on my relationship skills. I was better equipped to concentrate on supplementing our meager early retirement income.

The aerospace business was in a slump, so it was easier for me to start my own sales representative business than find a job. It gave us a lot of flexibility in time and the opportunity to travel between Santa Barbara and San Diego. We began to think about relocating. Our cross-country travels had made it clear to us that the only place for us was Southern California. We had not yet begun to ask God for His opinion, but ready or not He was about to jump into our plans.

Valerie had purchased a "guide to retirement housing", which she carried along during our business travels up and down the coast. About that time her mother, Mary, gave her a novena. Actually, it was more of a prayer chain letter. This came as quite a surprise since Mary, like me, was a cradle Catholic not prone to encourage people to pray outside of Sunday services. She was probably threatened by some unstated fear if she broke the chain. The novena uniquely stated that on the fourth day of this nine-day prayer, whatever you prayed for would be made clear. Valerie began her novena for guidance on our future home.

The fourth day we were driving home from San Diego. Valerie's book referred to Vista del Mar, a small senior community in the North County town of Vista. Following directions, we proceeded up a steep hill leading to our destination. At the top we turned left on Via del Mar. If we had been Bible study people at the time, we might have recognized the translation, "way of the sea", as a very significant road in the Old Testament. After passing a half dozen manufactured homes, we saw a "For Sale" sign on a single lot that backed up to a lovely grove of eucalyptus trees. In this charming community of about 250 homes, there stood one of the choicest lots, just waiting for us. I now believe that God put that lot in the hands of a Polish gentleman to hold for 13 years until we prayerfully came by. Please recall that me and the Pope are both Polish, or should that be the Pope and me?

I stopped the car, jumped out and ran up a slope at the back of the lot. From there I could see all the way to the Pacific Ocean, our own little "Vista del Mar." On the way down, the loose soil gave way, and I slid to the bottom on my clean white shorts. When we look at what comes later, the fall might be equated to St. Paul being knocked off his horse. We purchased the property that day, fully confident that this is where God meant us to be. It was probably my first real thought about God's plan for us. The plan became more obvious when we learned that the Catholic church, St. Francis of Assisi, was just a mile away.

It took a year before we would actually make the move. There was a house to sell and a new one to purchase and erect. We expected the sale would be difficult, considering that earlier that year our home had been near the center of the Northridge earthquake.

With God's help Californians were quick to forget. The house sold in a matter of weeks.

The most important consideration, at least to Valerie, was family. With the exception of our Las Vegas contingent, all the family lived north of Los Angeles. We would be putting another 120 miles between us. The kids would be fine, having their own lives, but her parents, although active, were now in their 80s. For me, well, I was still in the loaner Joe mode developed during my drinking. During the transition year we made many one-day trips back and forth to Vista and realized this was not a problem. Before Starbucks, Californians would drive 120 miles for a good cup of coffee. Besides, this is the place God chose for us.

It has been said that when you begin to get close to God, the opposition will start to interfere. In one of Frank Perreti's novels on spiritual warfare, the good Christian heroine is trying to escape from the bad guys. When she hops in her car and tries to drive off, one of satan's warriors sticks a finger in the engine, causing it to stall.

I'm reasonably certain that one of the evil henchmen was doing just that to our little motor home. Every time we headed to Vista with a load of possessions, the vehicle would stall about half way in the journey. Fortunately we were towing our baby blue 1980 Chevy Luv pick-up, which was able to take over and complete the trip. So, why did the devil not do his dastardly deeds on the truck? It may be due to prayer and our affection for what we called "Ole Blue." The most significant factor may have been Valerie dubbing it WWJD (what would Jesus drive). The mechanics were never able to solve the motor home problem that only manifested itself on the way to Vista. In spite of that, on the final day of our move, we tried it one more time.

By the time the movers, "Starving Jewish Students," had loaded their truck, it was getting dark. We put the last of our personal possessions in the RV, hooked up Ole Blue and headed south with much anxiety. God did not allow the evil one to deter us from His chosen destination. About midnight we arrived at the RV park we would call home for three weeks while the builders finished their work. In the morning, when ready to drive the 12 miles to see our new house, the RV would not start. Apparently God said, "Hey, I got you this far, you can handle the rest." So again we relied on Ole Blue.

When we no longer needed the RV for living quarters, AAA towed it to the service station nearest our home, where Ken and Donnie managed to get it running again. During the repair they discovered a small leak in the gas tank caused by the rubbing of a hot exhaust pipe. I guess The Lord wasn't ready for us yet.

Vista

By California standards, Vista is a small city, with a population of about eighty thousand. Regardless of the numbers, it is a small town in spirit. Even in the same large chain stores we had in Los Angeles, the employees are much warmer and more helpful. You can even buy the North County Times, our daily newspaper, on most major corners, not from young boys in knicker pants, but from grown men in blue hats who are working their way out of addiction.

The city is about forty miles north of San Diego and a short six miles from the Pacific Ocean. There is a country atmosphere once you are off the main highway, with rolling hills, numerous trees and flower nurseries coexisting with individual homes and small tracts. The main attractions make it sound like a farm community. Guajome Park boasts a renowned museum of antique tractors, steam engines and farm equipment. Rancho Guajome Adobe is an old Spanish villa that offers tours and special events like the annual quilt show and Civil War reenactment. The downtown includes a live theater, the Avo, and about a mile away is Brengle Terrace Park, home of The Moonlight Amphitheater. Residents can enjoy a picnic on the grass and a first-class Broadway play under the stars. Once a year St. Francis of Assisi Church holds its "Mass in the park" at the same location, where the night before, hundreds may have been enjoying "Phantom of the Opera."

Downtown Vista is currently undergoing a redevelopment, adding more restaurants, shops and a major movie theater chain. The residents are keeping a close eye to assure it doesn't interfere with the small town charm. The centerpiece of the new area will be a "creek walk", smaller but similar to the San Antonio "river walk." A few miles away is the county courthouse, surrounded by, of course, numerous law offices and fast food eateries.

And churches, lots and lots of churches of every denomination in every corner of the city, with more under construction. Probably the largest is the previously mentioned St. Francis, with over six thousand registered families. It offers an equal number of Spanish and English Masses, plus one in Vietnamese. With nine weekend Masses and only the pastor, Father Ramon, and one associate, it often becomes necessary to bring in priests from the surrounding churches. In Vista, this is not a problem. In addition to the many other Catholic parishes, within a few miles there is the Mission San Luis Rey, The Prince of Peace, Benedictine Abbey, plus a number of Indian reservation missions. Also, with what's touted as "the best climate in the country", Vista and the surrounding area is a frequent vacation and retirement location for a number of priests and religious.

Is it any wonder God chose this for our home? I've often thought that the air space over Vista should be declared a no-fly zone to avoid collision with the Holy Spirit and the celestial helpers.

We shall never forget our first Mass at St. Francis. As we entered the church, there was an overwhelming feeling of warmth and peace. We were truly home. On a number of occasions, especially during the monthly praise and worship Mass, I had experienced a faintness that forced me to sit down before I fell. Although I was not yet open to the Holy Spirit, I recognized the feeling as spiritual rather than a physical anomaly. It wasn't until much later that we would learn about "resting in the Spirit."

Probably the first of many minor miracles, or what we began calling God-incidences, occurred about a week after we moved in. Our good friends Chuck and Joan had lived in the San Diego area for several years. They were really good Christian people, although not necessarily associated with an organized religion. Joan was the first to visit us bearing a housewarming gift. First, you should realize that Joan knew little about our Catholic faith and nothing about the church we had settled into. Yet there she stood on our doorstep, holding a two-foot tall statue of St. Francis of Assisi. She admitted to knowing nothing about him but thought it to be an appropriate outdoor decoration for her religious friends. Apparently, our new neighbors and members of our parish, Dolores and Al, whom we had not yet met, were equally overjoyed to see this woman approach our house carrying the image of St. Francis. Reportedly Dolores yelled to her husband, "Praise God, they're Catholic."

Our new church being relatively close to our home was a real plus, for we were determined to become active in the parish. God immediately opened the door. In the first church bulletin we read, The St. Francis, Promise Keepers were publicizing a new members meeting and prayer breakfast on the following Saturday. To my knowledge there are very few Catholic parishes that embrace the Promise Keepers movement. I joined immediately.

Apparently there is a little known phenomenon of parish life, that once you join one organization, you become fair game for every other ministry. It must be like the indelible mark on the soul each time you receive a sacrament. Church volunteers must have an invisible "V" on their foreheads that can only be seen by ministry leaders. That brings up a point: if your marriage is annulled, what happens to the indelible mark???

Well, back to church. Unfortunately, it's a well-known fact that in any denomination of religion only about ten percent of the church population participates in any of the ministries. Everyone else attends services to get their ticket punched, the hope being that when we meet St. Peter, our ticket will have enough holes to qualify our admittance through the pearly gates. Ten percenters know there is much more to God's plan.

Promise Keepers was extremely beneficial, when I was able to make the meetings. The problem was, in order to accommodate the non-retired members, which was the majority, they met at 6:00 a.m. on Friday mornings. At my stage in life, I was reluctant to acknowledge that 6:00 came around twice in the same day. But for a couple of years I participated in that ritualistic sacrifice, and God rewarded us with more opportunities to serve.

The city of Vista is unique in another way – it has a heart. At the center of that heart was a gracious lady mayor by the name of Gloria. Every year, starting in about September, she and the city council debated the need for an emergency homeless shelter, to operate during the cold and rainy months. And every year, at the last minute, Gloria and enough council members agreed to funding, one more time. That's the way politicians work, even the few who sincerely want to help others. The North County Times faithfully reports all the shelter news, starting with the debates through the shelter closing in March or April. After that the whole process begins again.

For some unknown reason, when first I read about the program for the homeless, it called to me for participation. After the typical phone run-around associated with bureaucratic activities, I finally reached a very congenial gentleman named Rich, who was in charge of volunteers. I really just wanted to help, but by the end of our conversation I had agreed to furnish a group of six to work one night every two weeks. At that early stage I barely knew five other people in Vista.

The next Friday morning with sign-up sheet in hand I took my plea to the Promise Keepers meeting. Maybe it was the early morning mental fog, but most likely it was true Christian fellowship that encouraged participation. Out of only 20 members, we got enough signatures for two groups and a couple of spares. For about the next six or more years, PK provided a group of at least six men, women and children to the shelter every week. Between cooking, serving, and passing out clothes and blankets, we have had the honor to do what Jesus taught us.

Mayor Gloria died a few years ago. I figure she was too busy in flight training school to watch over the acting mayor and city council, so the shelter didn't get funded this year. But next year should be back to business as usual. The people voted in a pro-shelter mayor and a few positive council members, so the debate should be starting up soon. Seems like mayor Gloria has earned her wings and is circling over the council chambers. We may have to remind the police helicopters about that no-fly zone.

There are many other examples of the Christian nature of Vista. In addition to the emergency shelter, we now have a permanent, year-round, 50-bed shelter for families, plus another 120-bed facility under construction, all funded by the city, local churches and various government grants. Then there is the Alpha project, a haven for rehabilitating alcoholics and addicts. As mentioned, you can purchase the daily newspaper on many corners in Vista from the Alpha "hawkers." We enjoy getting the paper that way. It provides an opportunity to offer encouragement to those struggling with sobriety. If the traffic light permits, we sometime share our stories. Some days Valerie and I both come home with the same paper.

On one major corner of our town is The Catholic Charities, a large, white complex that includes a thrift store and emergency food supplies, plus other services like immigration help, job counseling and general assistance in helping those in need to cope with a life that they may not be prepared for. A number of the churches offer hearty meals in their soup kitchens to many, some with jobs that just don't pay enough to provide food and shelter. If you haven't noticed, our economy has gotten out of hand for all except the very rich. And, lest we forget, there is the "Birth Choice" office in nearby San Marcos. Here expectant mothers and fathers can get the help they need to keep their child from becoming a statistic at the nearest abortion chamber. Did I mention that almost all of the services mentioned above are free of charge and staffed by volunteers?

The biggest complaint voiced by some residents, merchants and politicians is that all this generosity simply encourages those needing help to seek it in our city. That is probably true, but if you're looking to follow the example of Jesus, Vista might just be the place to start, for if we keep our hearts open, *"the poor we will always have with us."*

The Holy Spirit Speaks

There are so many elements contributing to my conversion that it's difficult to identify some as more important than others, but this rates near or at the top. As we began checking out the various daily Masses, it wasn't long before we came upon The Prince of Peace Abbey. This beautiful monastery and retreat complex sits on a hill above Oceanside with a spectacular view of the Pacific Ocean. Mass with the congregation of Benedictine monks is a marvelously solemn celebration.

Afterward we followed the regulars over to the hospitality center and gift shop for a cup of coffee and a loaf of fresh baked bread. There isn't much available for free these days and certainly nothing of real value, but there on a table sat a generous supply of free books and pamphlets. The one that caught my attention was a small, yellowish-orange booklet titled "Novena to the Holy Spirit." Considering that I had never been a repetitive prayer person, it's difficult to explain this one grabbing me, but it did, and I took a copy home.

The next morning I began the prayer ritual that would continue for years and change my life forever. Even though I was just reading the words printed on paper, God began to open my heart and my mind to something I could not understand for some time.

This was also my first exposure to the seven gifts of the Holy Spirit:

Wisdom
Knowledge
Understanding
Counsel
Fortitude
Piety
Fear of the Lord

Piety, I believe, was the first I actually experienced. It manifested as an extreme peacefulness unlike anything I had ever felt. It was this gift that I first witnessed to in a public sharing on faith. As a salesman I gave many talks, but never on a religious subject I knew little about.

At the end of the reading for the ninth day, the novena encourages you to start over again, "a perpetual novena," and so I did, day after day, year after year. I began to order bulk quantities of the little book to pass out to anyone who would listen. The Holy Spirit had me evangelizing without yet knowing the meaning of the word. It wasn't until I was deep into Holy Scripture that the Spirit allowed me to set aside the novena and move on to a deeper search for understanding God.

Even though we participated in the SCRC (Southern California Renewal Communities) Labor Day weekends with fifteen thousand charismatic Catholics plus our monthly praise and worship Mass, I was still waiting to be "zapped" by the Holy Spirit. Valerie had experienced "resting in the Spirit," but I remained upright and clear headed even after being touched by some of God's most powerful healers. It appears I just wasn't ready to fully let go.

When St. Francis' charismatic group put on a week-long "Life in the Spirit" seminar, I figured this was going to be the life changing experience I was seeking. Many people shared about the gifts they had received, but I was disappointed again. Well, not completely. It appeared that the Spirit had allowed me the "Gift of Tongues." I'm unsure what was expected, but even that was not enough.

I didn't give up and neither did the Holy Spirit. There was a significant change that I did not recognize, for somewhere in those early years in Vista, I had quit saying and feeling "is that all there is?" I knew there was more to come.

Byways to Heaven

We continued our RV travels, although not as extensively as in 1992. One of our favorite annual trips is a late January drive to Quartzsite, Arizona, home of the "worlds largest swap meet and flea market." Every January through March this little town of 2,000 residents swells to over a million, most of us living in RVs. There are stands of various shapes, sizes and colors stretching for miles along Business Route 10. The vendors are ready to buy, sell or trade almost anything you can imagine. We did notice, however, a distinct lack of religious items, and yet the Queen of Peace Catholic Church is filled to overflowing at the single weekend Mass. I'm sure this is also true of the half dozen other churches in the area. Some of the RV parks hold non-denominational services on Sunday mornings. It seemed obvious that there was a need not being satisfied, and so we founded Byways to Heaven. The business was to be a Christian book and gift store on wheels.

His Plan -- My Conversion

Shortly after we registered the DBA in San Diego County, God, we thought, made his presence felt again. Needing some service on our little RV, we were steered to a very special shop in North County called <u>Son</u> Rise RV. Don, the owner, was always anxious to witness about his faith to anyone who would listen. He even had a box of miniature Bibles for the taking. Valerie noticed a shiny 1990 class A motor home for sale at the curb. It was what is called a basement model, with lots of storage for the wares of our new business. Don had it on consignment and assured us that it was in excellent condition. After a few discernment prayers plus a couple of financial calculations, we stepped up to a 30-foot traveling business rig. We immediately stopped at the DMV for new license plates, "TO HEAV'N", and then to a local sign shop that added in large script on the back, *Let Us Pray For You.*

A most humorous reaction to our evangelization efforts came from my "cradle Catholic" father-in-law, Harvey. After looking at the back end of our new RV, he said with all sincerity, "You're sure getting into this religious crap." He was obviously going to be a tough sell, or as his son puts it, "Harv's a tough out."

It wasn't long before we had to admit that just maybe, Discernment was one charism with which we had not yet been blessed. It appears that our desire for a larger motor home, coupled with a hope for more travel, may have distracted us from God's plan. Most authorities on divine decision making talk of three types of spiritual guidance: the Holy Spirit, what we asked for; the evil spirit, which God protects us from; and of course our own human wants and wishes. For whatever reason, the business never got rolling. Byways to Heaven instead became our personal ministry.

It's good to have a ministry, complete with business cards and stationary. Everyone takes notice, and we have been asked numerous times to pray for others along the road. It's a wonderful opportunity to witness and evangelize, even though, at first, I had trouble explaining exactly what we do. The ministry continues today, even though it still lacks complete definition. Maybe that's where God took over, because it's a vibrant, growing thing that has led us to fascinating people and places, all of which have been positive, and most of all, our relationship with the true CEO continues to flourish.

One Bread, One Body

It became obvious that between Vista, St. Francis Parish, and the novena to the Holy Spirit, life was changing. I was beginning to think about God in my everyday life. Not constantly, but enough to get my attention.

One day my neighbor, Al, gave us copies of a little booklet titled, "One Bread, One Body" (OBOB). It was not unlike the numerous daily meditation pamphlets that Christians have been reading for years. It lists the Scripture readings for each day followed by a brief meditation, plus prayer, promise and praise notes. But that's where the similarity ends. Whenever we pass out copies of OBOB, I am quick to caution the recipient that it is "not for the faint of heart." It is not a "feel good" message, assuring the reader of their guaranteed place in Heaven. Father Al Lauer, who wrote 99 percent of the meditation, calls us to live life according to the teachings and example of Jesus, without exception. He also emphasizes the importance of being docile to the Holy Spirit and submissive to the teachings of the Magestarium, while encouraging frequent, if not daily, participation in the Eucharistic celebration. Father Al recognizes his approach to faith as radical, especially when contrasted with the watered down Christianity fostered by our "culture of death." OBOB quickly became a critical part of our daily prayer ritual. I began to notice that the daily Bible readings and Father Al's meditations often spoke to me about a subject I was pondering at the time. But at this point my understanding of the gifts of the Holy Spirit (charisms), such as prophecy, was still seriously lacking.

We will take a much more detailed look at OBOB in future chapters, for it was truly another of the major elements in my conversion over a period of years. For now, let's move on to another of God's minor miracles, or we will never get to Phoebe.

Little Rock Scripture Study

(LRSS)

A few months later a notice appeared in the church bulletin inviting interested parishioners to an open meeting. The topic was the start of a parish Bible study program. There were a number of small prayer groups meeting regularly to read and discuss Scripture, but there was no designated ministry or leadership. A few volunteers had investigated available studies including the "Little Rock Scripture Study."

At the time we were starting, LRSS was the largest Catholic Bible study, already in existence for about twenty years. To Valerie and me it sounded ideal. It was touted as being for beginners as well as experienced Scripture students, and it required no expert teachers, simply facilitators. Even though out of 15,000 parishioners, there were no more than one hundred at this initial meeting, they were an enthusiastic group. Apparently none was more excited than I, who made the mistake of asking a question, "What do we do now?" A couple of hours after returning home, we received a call from the parish office, asking us to head up the new St. Francis Bible study. For some reason, with little hesitation, we said yes. In a very, very small way, I knew how Mary felt after saying yes to the angel of God.

Who were we to run this program for one of the largest Catholic parishes? Neither of us had read Scripture on a regular basis, much less tried to understand it. The lesson here is, never ask a question at a church meeting, unless you want a lifetime commitment. Just kidding! Learning to listen to God's word, which is what Scripture is, may be the single most significant factor in my spiritual journey. I'm sure God has spoken to me in the past – I just didn't know how to listen. With the help of two other volunteers and the guidance of our Irish leprechaun, Sister Madeline Fitzgerald, we managed to round up enough potential facilitators for about twelve small groups. There would be Little Rock groups meeting mornings, afternoon and evenings, most days of the week. No one could say, "I can't make it that day," although many still try.

And so we started with about one hundred eager participants, and seven years later we still have about the same number. Each new session brings new members, while an equal number drop out. I'd hate to report to St. Peter with an incomplete in Bible study on my life's report card. The majority have stuck with the program over its span. At one point in 1999 we got up to 150 members for the study of "The Book of Revelation." Everyone wanted to know if the world was going to end with the new millennium. It didn't.

The numbers may be small when you consider the size of the St. Francis population, but even Jesus spoke about how few workers there were in the vineyard. That's why some of us are blessed to spread the Good News and try to make disciples of all nations. If it was all that easy, we might not need all the help God so willingly offers.

It still bothers me a little, and so each year I try a new publicity campaign. Then I reflect on the words of Mother Teresa: "God didn't call me to be successful, just faithful." But there is success, maybe not in the numbers, but in the individuals who thirst for the Word, year after year. Probably the best example is my neighbor Al. Prior to joining LRSS, due to limited opportunity for education, he considered himself a non-reader. Now every day with Bible, concordance, and two dictionaries, he spends hours preparing for the next lesson. Along with his wife, Dolores, they have become our co-facilitators and take over whenever we are traveling.

I often feel the greatest beneficiaries of our LRSS program at St. Francis have to be Valerie and me. We are now anxious to share, with anyone who will listen, the importance of studying Scripture. Although we pray that all of our participants are equally blessed by the

Holy Spirit, I feel a reward I would have never thought possible. But, *"with God, all things are possible."* The reason the numbers still bother me is because I can't imagine anyone following the Father, Son and Holy Spirit without listening to the Word. But that was me just about six or seven years ago.

Two final and most significant notes on reading Scripture: Pray before and after each reading. Following are the prayers we use:

Opening Prayer

>Open my heart, Holy Spirit,
>to receive Your word
>and enlighten my mind
>to understand it.
>Strengthen me, Holy Spirit,
>to follow wherever You lead.

Closing Prayer

>I thank You, Holy Spirit,
>for your word.
>Make it a living reality in my life,
>a constant guide at my side,
>a lamp for my feet
>and a light for my path.
>Let it mold my mind
>and shape my heart
>into the image of Christ, my Lord
>and in conformity to Your holy will.

And, when you begin to recognize, as I do, God speaking to you, through Scripture, about your day-to-day life, then you are truly communicating with Him, and that is the goal. Later I will share some of the hundreds of times God has spoken directly to me, but it's time to introduce Phoebe.

Phoebe

If you're keeping score at home, my morning prayer now includes: The Novena to the Holy Spirit, One Bread, One Body, Scripture readings for the day, plus additional Scripture and commentary in preparation for the next session of LRSS, and, oh yes, a few miscellaneous prayers.

Let's see if I can set the scene. My prayer chair is next to a sliding glass door that overlooks the patio. At the end of this 15 feet of concrete is a 4-foot high retaining wall topped with a 5-foot chain link fence. Inside the fence is the statue of St. Francis and our shrine to the Blessed Mother. On the other side is a beautiful grove of tall willowy eucalyptus trees. This designated green area is another blessing that came with the city of Vista. Every morning I sit and stare and praise the Father for the wonder of His creation, especially the little share He has placed just outside our backyard. Some days the Southern California sun is streaming through the trees. Other days there is the May gray or June gloom, fog of the coastal region. Regardless, it's always beautiful and worthy of praise and thanksgiving. Of course, with the trees comes an assortment of birds, including ravens (some might call them crows), doves, mockingbirds, sparrows and warblers, plus an occasional red tail hawk or horned owl.

I'm not sure when it started, maybe long before I first noticed, but one morning there appeared on the fence between St. Francis and Mary a small charcoal black bird with a white belly and wing tips. It stayed for just a moment and then disappeared. A few days later our visitor appeared again, during prayer time, and quickly vanished. When Valerie joined me in our prayer area, I commented on the new species in our backyard. She admitted to recently noticing the same phenomena, also during a time of meditation. We quickly got out our reference card of local birds and discovered our new caller to be a Black Phoebe.

Our larger bird book provided more details. For example, the Phoebe's call is a "sharp down slurred chirp," which she uses frequently when we don't immediately notice her presence. The habitat is defined as "shady areas near water; streams, ponds and lake banks." Our green area qualifies as shady, but we are at least six miles from the nearest water. Phoebes are indigenous to an area from "northern California south and east to western Texas", which doesn't explain her appearance in a shrine to Mary outside of St. Louis, Missouri.

We began to take Phoebe's visits as an affirmation that we were doing something acceptable to God, good works if you will. She became known by us as a representative of the Holy Spirit, but why a Black Phoebe??? After all, we have lots of doves in the backyard. Is not that species the official Biblical delegate of God's Spirit? It would be several months before we received the answer.

In preparation for another extended RV trip, I told – you might say threatened – Valerie of my intention to get a crewcut, like I had in high school. She was less than enthusiastic, since, for one thing, it adds emphasis to my larger-than-normal size ears. Women are funny that way about their husbands' appearance. So I told her I would pray on it. Actually, I had no intention of bothering God with such a mundane matter, even though He does know exactly *how many hairs there are on my head*. But what does that have to do with Phoebe? Glad you asked.

Shortly thereafter I was reading through some of the documents from Vatican II. One of them led me to "St. Paul's Letter to the Romans," chapter 16, verses 1 and 2: *"I commend to you Phoebe, our sister, who is (also) a minister of the church at Cenchrea, that you may receive her in the Lord, in a manner worthy of holy ones, and help her in whatever she may need from you, for she has been a benefactor to many and to me as well."*

Wanting to know more, I looked up Cenchrea, which referred me to Acts 18:18: *"Paul remained for quite some time, and after saying farewell to the brothers he sailed for Syria. At Cenchrea he got a crewcut (my interpretation), because he had taken a vow."* Apparently Paul didn't have a wife or large ears. My hair remains long.

The biblical references plus numerous other events convinced Valerie and me that Phoebe is truly a representative of the Holy Spirit, and we tell everyone about her. A spiritual gift is given for the benefit of the community. She continues to appear and will be mentioned throughout the remainder of this book.

For now, though out of sequence, let me share a few significant visits. It's not always obvious to us exactly why we are blessed with Phoebe's arrival. For the most part, as mentioned, we take it as affirmation for being involved with God's work. The most apparent of these is during times of prayer and meditation.

Phoebe invariably makes her presence known when we are working on the start of our next Bible study. One Sunday, about 6:30 a.m., I was on my way to church to set up the Little Rock registration tables. Suddenly our feathered advocate began flying back and forth in front of the car and continued for about a mile or two. It helped me to recognize the importance of my task, which had not seemed that exciting, especially considering the early hour. Later that same morning when I offered assistance to a homeless lady pushing a shopping cart with all her possessions past the church, Phoebe chirped her approval and did another fly-by.

Sometimes after a difference of opinion (argument to some), Valerie and I sit out on the patio and discuss all our blessings. Many times we are interrupted by that persistent chirp, which seems to be saying, I'm glad you got that out of your system.

Some appearances may not always be affirmations. During a visit from my in-laws, Harvey, of "religious crap" fame, plopped down in my prayer chair next to the window. Immediately Phoebe came and began darting in and out, up and down, all over the patio. Harvey asked, "What's with the crazy bird?" This gave us the opportunity to share about our personal representative from the Holy Spirit. Harvey's response was something between humbug and a grunt. Phoebe put on the same type of flying demonstration for one of our visiting adult children, who had drifted away from his faith. This time, our explanation met with at least mild acceptance.

Then there are times when I don't have a clue what the Holy Spirit is trying to tell us. I had taken the RV to our local wooded campground for a couple of days of cleaning and polishing in preparation for a trip. During a relaxation break, I noticed our black and white friend flying in my direction. The closer she got, the faster she flew. Finally, about two feet from my face, Phoebe did a sharp swerving maneuver; it nearly knocked me off my chair. Like I said, "Not a clue."

I pray that some of you begin to accept that there is a presence with Phoebe beyond that of a small, friendly bird. Later we'll discuss some of the more dramatic manifestations of the Holy Spirit. This is not an isolated phenomenon, and others have shared our close encounter with God's representatives, and, yes, there have even been a few other acknowledgments of His appearance in bird form. A group of about thirty men watched a small bluebird peck away at our chapel window every day of our Cursillo weekend. Hundreds of people, during a retreat on the charisms of the Holy Spirit, noticed a small dark bird, continually flying, as if trying to enter through the high, clear glass church windows. Perhaps it was Phoebe. Keep a close eye as God strives to make His presence known to everyone.

The Year of the Holy Spirit

Leading up to the new millennium, the Pope had declared the prior three years to honor and bring attention to the Trinity (another of God's mysteries of which I had zero knowledge or understanding, other than what I received at Sacred Heart of Mary Elementary School). I nearly missed 1997, the year of Jesus. My conversion was still in its infancy. 1998, the year of the Holy Spirit, was exactly that for me. I went into it as a lion of enthusiasm for our new home and surroundings and came out a lamb ready to be led by the Good Shepherd.

One Bread, One Body continued to be an inspiration for me to a holier life. The daily Scripture passages coupled with Father Al's writings were beginning to challenge my life in a way I did not comprehend. Ideas about my faith journey filtered through my thoughts, even with my lack of charisms such as wisdom, knowledge or understanding. I prayed slightly more fervently for these gifts, even though I didn't know the distinction between them. I prayed also for fortitude so that I would not slip back from wherever God was leading me.

An insert in the middle of OBOB described the upcoming summer retreat series and Bible Institute, all based, naturally, on the Holy Spirit. I suggested to Valerie that it might be an interesting adventure, as we had never been to the Cincinnati area. Her response was the same as most beach area dwellers when confronted with the opportunity to spend a summer in the heat and humidity of the Midwest. Even though I graciously accepted her "no thank you," I did not completely forget the idea.

That Friday, I dragged my body out of bed in time to make the 6:00 a.m. Promise Keepers gathering. I was no longer a regular in the group, primarily due to the early hour. My first encounter was a man named Bill whom I had met briefly, just once before. After our mutual re-introduction, he startled me with, "Joe, you should go to the Bible Institute."

After the initial shock wore off, I asked Bill the reason for his comment. He responded with, "I really don't know, it just came to me." I probably couldn't see Phoebe circling above the meeting hall. When I got home, I immediately relayed the details to Valerie, who continued the morning of surprises with an almost casual, "Well, I guess we should go." Before either of us could have second thoughts, I phoned Presentation Ministries and reserved one of their three RV parking spots. Vivian, who took my call, was thrilled at the prospect of attendees all the way from San Diego. As for me, although not knowing what was in store, I was elated and a bit apprehensive about 40 days of retreat.

As we prepared for the trip, we prayed for guidance in our travel. When you ask God for advice, it would make sense to follow wherever He leads. But this was one of the few occasions we did not, and I still wonder about the impact.

Since we were deeply involved with the Little Rock Scripture Study, we considered visiting their offices in Arkansas. The plan was to pick up promotional material to encourage Scripture study in the many parishes we visited along the way. Another stop we pondered was at the Eternal Word Television Network (EWTN) just outside Birmingham, Alabama. With my sales and marketing background, I would offer help to Mother Angelica in publicizing our only Catholic TV channel. To me, they were seriously lacking in promotion.

In response to our discernment prayers, God did not specifically say: *go to Little Rock* or *go to Birmingham*. It took a little faith and a bit of the charism of understanding, but that's how He works. A meditation from OBOB referred us to Jeremiah, chapter 2, verse 16, *"the people of Memphis."* Now Memphis, Tennessee is just about half way between the other two destinations. For both of us that was close enough. So I quickly dropped a line to LRSS and EWTN announcing our plans to grace them with

His Plan -- My Conversion

our presence, to which I'm sure they said *WHO???* As seasoned travelers, we monitored the TV and radio for weather forecasts. The word out of both Arkansas and Alabama was not good; temperatures in excess of 100 degrees were predicted for the foreseeable future, and so we opted for a more northerly route. Maybe if we had followed His instructions, Byways to Heaven just might have been the first Catholic multimedia giant. Only God knows.

However, the altered plans took us through St. Louis, Missouri and the spiritual highlight of the drive to Ohio. We stopped in a KOA off highway 44. While I checked in, Valerie went through the brochure rack of local tourist traps. Unlike the attractions we are accustomed to, particularly in California, she came across a brochure on a nearby shrine to the Black Madonna, the first and only Catholic travel guide we had ever encountered, and so we elected to search it out. Finding the location was as easy as finding the pamphlet, for it was less than a mile from the campground. Another God incidence??? We think so.

The shrine includes a "true copy of the world-famous miraculous picture of Our Lady of Czetochowa." Tradition tells us that St. Luke painted it on the top of the cypress wood table that was built by St. Joseph and used by the Holy Family at Nazareth, and that Mary sat for the painting. The grottos surrounding the main outdoor chapel are made of rocks, seashells and bits of jewelry. They are dedicated to the stations of the cross, the seven joys of Mary, St. Francis, St. Joseph, Our Lady of Perpetual Help, Our Lady of Sorrows, the Assumption, the Nativity and the garden of Gethsemane. Inside the chapel near the painting is a statue of St. Joseph with one outstretched arm. His finger is extended as if to be pointing.

As we approached the statue, Valerie excitedly called my attention to another of God's minor miracles. There sitting on the finger of my patron saint in a shrine devoted to a Polish Lady was Phoebe, in all her glory. Recalling your earlier ornithology lesson, the species is indigenous to the west and as far east as western Texas. Maybe the turn north wasn't our decision. When I discuss the year 2000, we will address pilgrimages versus trips or vacations. At this point we didn't know how special a religious journey could be. A homily we once heard said, "When you are truly on a pilgrimage, expect miracles."

We traversed the final 75 miles east from Cincinnati to our ultimate destination, Peebles, Ohio, the type of place mentioned in the back section of the AAA guide only because it has a motel. Travelers would get off the highway here for gas or a McDonalds hamburger. For us it would be our home for the next 30 days.

The Discipleship Center was several miles from the town in an area of farms lightly sprinkled with new homes, obviously for those wanting to get away from the thriving metropolis. The property had been donated to Presentation Ministries (PM) by a devout Catholic

His Plan -- My Conversion

widow named Vivian Jansen from part of a large farm she had owned with her husband. Apparently, they had been active in beginning PM, and he had always envisioned a retreat house on this location.

As our RV strained up a long, steep, private dirt road, we could see a giant cross at the top. On the right was the Jansen family home, and straight ahead, as we crested the hill, was a large very plain structure which included a combination hall, chapel, kitchen and limited living quarters. The majority of the retreat attendees were housed in cabins and old classroom trailers scattered throughout the lush green property. Some of the rooms had plumbing, and one even had air conditioning. Father Al's cabin was the most remote and spartan of the lot, which describes his lifestyle. We would learn later that he did not own a car, and if one was not available to borrow, he often hitchhiked the 75 miles to his parish in Cincinnati and back. Fortunately, our motor home included all of what we come to call the necessities, especially since our parking area contained what RVers call full hook-ups.

The welcoming and parking committee included Vivian, Carl, who maintained most of the facility, and his wife Judy. The rest we could meet later at Sunday night supper or the following morning, the official start of our retreat. Probably because of a certain amount of useless anxiety, we declined the meal and opted to spend one last evening together in our RV. Our hosts were obviously disappointed, since we were no longer visitors but members of a "Small Christian Community" called "Holy Mountain."

Our first Monday in Peebles began, as would each of the next thirty days, with the Liturgy of the Hours, followed by Mass and breakfast. It was at this time that we met the man who previously we knew only from his writings. Father Al was a tall, slender man who would celebrate his 50th birthday while we were there. He was truly a holy man, as epitomized by his humility and devotion to Jesus Christ. Unlike many retreat directors in out-of-the-way locations, Father Al always wore his priestly garb. During our introduction, we learned that Father Al had actually visited Vista about a year before we moved to the area. He had been invited to stop at our church and discuss the possibility of conducting a parish mission. A change of pastors took place at St. Francis, and the whole idea was put on hold.

The retreat program included many one-, two- and three-day talks, all centered, of course, around the Holy Spirit. The Holy Mountain community members attended every lecture. Many, like us, were there for the first time, some for the entire series, but others drifted in and out, particularly on weekends. The numbers fluctuated between thirty and forty. Almost everyone was a long-term follower of Father Al through OBOB. Some had formed their own small Christian communities with names like Acts 2:42, New Creations and Servant. Attendees came from Ohio and surrounding states, plus another lady from

Orange County, California, a couple from Florida, and even a few from out of the country. We were also blessed to have Father John, who was on sabbatical and would be relocating to New Mexico. He added his own brand of holiness in discussion plus filling in at Mass. Although we had an occasional visiting speaker, Father Al conducted about ninety-five percent of the lectures. What a blessing! It was probably the last retreat with that much participation from the leader.

Other than his humility, I would describe our retreat master as a shy man in social situations. Like me, it was obvious he had little use for small talk. Father Al's demeanor changed drastically, however, as he began to lecture. Even with his humble nature and relatively quiet voice, he, like the apostles, was filled with the gifts of the Holy Spirit and ready to make disciples of anyone who wandered into his presence. Every day for about four hours, plus a homily during Mass, Father Al shared the gifts using only a small, well worn Bible that was always in his hands. Each and every day we in the audience were mesmerized by the Word of God as given through this holy man.

We began with a "Life in the Spirit Seminar" and went on to examine such topics as:

The Holy Spirit and Evangelization
Gifts of the Spirit
Lifestyles in the Spirit
The Holy Spirit Makes Disciples
How the Spirit builds Christian Community

It is impossible to adequately relay the impact of the talks. Most people, including cradle Catholics, would prefer not to hear the message, just as many rebelled against the teachings of our savior. Later in Part 2, I will attempt to share insights from the over one hundred pages of notes taken during the retreat and Bible Institute.

Every day brought a new challenge to grow in faith and love while realizing that "*we are not of this world.*" Even though the message was directly from Scripture, many will have difficulty accepting this relationship to worldly teaching. It appeared that everyone listening chose to believe. There was no question that all we were taught was in full agreement with the Bible, Sacred Tradition and the Magestarium. It was like being present at the "Sermon on the Mount." Never will we hear these words again in the same way until, hopefully, we are in the presence of Jesus Christ.

The structure of the retreat did not allow for a lot of quiet meditation time. That would take place after we returned home. In addition to the Liturgy of the Hours four times a day and Mass, there was an afternoon rosary and divine mercy chaplet. Of course, there was the three abundant meals. Like the early Christians, we all participated in the preparation, serving and clean-up. It was a whole new way of life for many and especially for me, the loaner.

There was an obvious biblical composition to the time in Ohio, starting with the significant 40 days

(Retreat plus Bible Institute). If you completed the entire program, there was an anointing and the participants were given a scapular, symbolic of Elijah putting his cloak over his disciple Elisha. At an earlier ceremony, we were presented with a necklace consisting of a small wooden cross on a leather thong, as a sign of our discipleship. Six years later I still wear that cross daily, to witness. It has given me numerous opportunities to share my faith. There have also been many questioning glances and even a few queries as to whether I am a man of the cloth, to which I respond, "No, a Disciple." If you have trouble evangelizing, as I still do, try wearing a simple wooden cross (mine is 3 inches high) over your clothing and see what happens.

I recall that on the final day of the retreats, Father Al asked if there were any questions or comments. I responded by thanking him, inadequately, for the wonderful thirty days and then asked, "Now that you have given us these truths, what are we to do with them?" I don't recall getting an answer, and it is a question I will probably ponder for the rest of my life. One obvious reply might have been, *go forth and make disciples of all nations.*

After the initial thirty days, we relocated to a more citified RV park on the outskirts of Cincinnati, and for the next 10 days we commuted to the campus of Xavier University for the Bible Institute. This annual event drew hundreds of PM followers to a structured series of lectures and classes, again, all centered on

The Year of the Holy Spirit

"The Year of The Holy Spirit." Along with Father Al and Archbishop Daniel Pilarczyk, there were guest speakers, including Ralph Martin, Catholic author and TV show host on EWTN.

As our primary course, both Valerie and I chose to spend the first five days learning "How To Teach The Bible," a natural for our parish ministry. Each time we begin a new Little Rock Scripture Study session, one of the first questions posed is "*who is the teacher.*" Though we explain that the leaders are facilitators, participants expect some sort of credential. Ten days at Xavier University can't hurt. There were about thirty participants in the Bible teaching course. We chose The Gospel According to Mark for this exercise. As with everything else about these 40 days, the instructor emphasized prayer and discernment through the Holy Spirit. Yes, let the Spirit guide your teaching. It Works!!!

As a reward for attentiveness and hard work, on the last day our instructor held a drawing. The prize was a beautiful framed crucifix donated by one of the students. Before he reached in the hat, Valerie interrupted with a suggestion. She noted that as we walked around the college campus, it was obvious that there was a severe lack of Catholic symbols. Except for the chapel, you would assume this was a secular institution. The building we were in housed the university president's office, which, as near as we could see, had no crucifix or pictures of Jesus, not even a picture of St. Xavier. Valerie's suggestion was to donate our prize to the president of the university. Several agreed, but others wanted the chance to win the impressive gift. A compromise was reached when we agreed to add a slip for the college to our lottery. With 30-1 odds, St. Xavier won the drawing. We all concluded that the prize went where it was needed most. Sometime, when you pray for discernment, the Holy Spirit just will make the right thing happen, against all odds.

At the end of 10 + 30 days, the anointing ceremony was held. Unfortunately Valerie and I did not qualify, as we had missed one retreat weekend to visit an aging aunt in nearby Illinois. Although it was probably the Christian thing, God may have questioned our motives, since she is supposedly very wealthy. I still wonder what special graces we missed and how much more could we evangelize with a scapular and a cross.

You may be surprised to hear that Phoebe didn't appear to have made the trip from Missouri to Ohio. When I was a sales representative, we had very specific territories to cover, and maybe that was the case here. Father Al may have been the exclusive rep in Ohio. It may also explain why he never got to complete his mission in Vista.

On the 10-day drive home, we took the opportunity for quiet time, praying, meditating and discussing what shall we do with our new gifts. One thing we agreed on was that the time for taking it all in should pass and we must concentrate on sharing the wonders of life in the Spirit, although we knew not how or where. Some people continue learning all their lives and continue praying for direction. We knew that God would show us the way if we showed faith by participating in His plan, day by day.

Another confirmation we had on the way home was the understanding that the closer we get to God, the more we open our hearts, the more the devil attempts to derail the journey. Not wanting to give the evil one too much credit or publicity, let me share only one somewhat humorous example of his manifestation.

We have, in our home and our RV, indoor/outdoor thermometers with large digital displays. Since moving to Vista we had noticed, on occasion, the displays registering the devil's numbers *66.6*, when it appeared that the actual temperature was much higher or lower. Being naive, we attributed the error to faulty equipment.

However, on the way from Peebles to San Diego, we noticed that number pattern more and more frequently. With our newfound knowledge and the Holy Spirit's guidance, we began to realize that this might well be a threat. Valerie suggested that each time it occurred we counter by repeatedly praying the name of Jesus. It seemed to help, as the numbers would change, but sometime we met greater resistance.

Digital thermometers are typically small, lightweight devices affixed to the wall with a small strip of Velcro. Being a belt and suspenders type person, mine was attached in the RV with two pieces of Velcro plus a large wad of earthquake putty to absorb the road vibration. That proved to be a successful combination for thousands of miles.

One day as we were parked for lunch, the unwanted numbers appeared, and our prayers were not producing the desired affect. I grabbed the holy water and lightly sprinkled the thermometer. Instantly the white plastic case shook repeatedly and fell from the wall, Velcro, putty and all. The numbers displayed had changed drastically.

We still encounter the repetitive sequence both at home and on the road, and we still pray the name of our Savior. It doesn't seem to be as frequent, and our concern has diminished as our faith and acts grow. We do make it a practice to have every new car, RV and home blessed by a priest. Like the holy water fonts at our front doors, it may be an old-fashioned sign of our belief, but we'll take all of God's protection we can get.

What Do We Do With the Truth?

We arrived home safe, happy and refreshed, ready to answer God's call. The line was open more than ever before. Just having gone on a 40-day retreat was enough witness for most people, and we told everyone who would listen. The most frequent response was *WOW!!*; the second most frequent was *WOW!!! I wish we could do that*. Of course, we continued to distribute OBOB plus the hundreds of Father Al books and pamphlets we brought back. We also returned with over one hundred tapes covering every lecture attended.

Anxious to share my newfound wisdom, I approached the men's ministry group at our parish. They were busy planning the annual weekend retreat, which was only two months off. After telling them about our 40 days, I offered to speak on some aspect of the truths we had learned. In spite of their *WOW*-full response, it did not fit with their theme, and it was too late for a change. About a week later the head of the ministry called. They had decided to take me up on my offer to

His Plan -- My Conversion

speak, but it must fit the overall program. Knowing about my recovery from alcoholism, they proposed a 45-minute talk on using God's grace to overcome addiction. I excitedly accepted my first invitation for a full-blown, evangelization opportunity.

It wasn't until I began to compose my thoughts that the significance of a long talk to over one hundred men came to me. It was frightening. In sales, I had given numerous product presentations, but nothing even close to a talk about God. So I did what every good Christian should do – I panicked and turned it over to Him. When finally I sat down at the computer to type, the words just flowed with little or no real thought from me. In a relatively short period, I had completed 20 pages. When Valerie read the first and only draft, it brought tears to her eyes. She insisted on making copies for family and friends, especially for those who were battling their own demons.

My talk, one of three, was scheduled first, right after breakfast on Saturday morning. I was too shaky to eat, so I wandered around the retreat grounds, praying and reviewing the speech in my mind. Suddenly there was that sharp, familiar chirp. I looked around for my black and white supporter but could not spot her amongst the many trees and shrubs. So I moved on a little further, and again the chirp, but no siting. This is a game she sometimes plays. Finally, after the third chirp, I saw Phoebe at the highest point of the tallest tree. While thanking God for this visit, suddenly the heavy weight of concern was lifted from mind and body. I was at peace, ready and anxious to get on with the presentation.

At the start, I asked the audience to extend their hands and pray that my speaking and their hearing would be what God wanted. Then I began with the official AA greeting: "Hi, I'm Joe and I'm an alcoholic." There were enough 12-steppers present for a hearty response, "Hi, Joe." There is another tradition at AA meetings, that members who have achieved one or more years of sobriety are presented a birthday cake. Since my anniversary date, October 22, was just a couple of days hence, I invited everyone to share the celebration complete with one candle for each of my seven years. The other AA members present led the Happy Birthday song, ending with the special closing line: "Keep Coming Back."

For about the next ten minutes I described what it was like being addicted and how easy God had made my cure. Then the talk covered many other types of addictions, such as money, TV, pornography, food, sex, cars and – probably the newest – the Internet. Listeners were surprised to learn that there are 12-step groups meeting on most of these problems. On the lighter side I mentioned my friend, who after overcoming drugs, had to start a new 12-step for Oreo cookies.

In the final segment, I admitted for the first time what is probably my most damaging addiction – ego! God has given me many blessings, but often I attribute success to my own ability rather than acknowledging the gifts of the Holy Spirit. So in an effort to overcome this sinful weakness, I closed with the following: "If you wish to discuss your addiction, please seek me out. But if you enjoyed or benefited from this talk, please help with my prideful addiction by honoring my request: please, no applause and no congratulatory comments." Almost everyone complied. The primary exception was Father Bob, the spiritual director. After listening to confessions for several hours, he approached at the end of the day with the revelation that my talk had inspired many men to come to him for forgiveness from their sins of addiction. Suddenly the reason for my alcoholism cross became not just clear, but a method for praising God.

I'm sure no one else noticed, but at the end of the closing Mass in the outdoor amphitheater, Phoebe, a single, solitary, small, black and white bird did a dramatic fly-over under God's beautiful sky.

Valerie was also spurred into action by our experience in Ohio. We both recognized the significance and looked for ways to expand our service. It is truly one of God's great blessings to share one's life with a person of exceptional faith. She had already encountered one conversion, when her husband, Ken, became a new and very enthusiastic Catholic. So to her the magnification of my faith was another confirmation of God's saving grace. We grew, not just in faith, but in our acts as well.

Together we acknowledged that it was time for more than just learning.

Needing discernment on many issues, we began a ritual of daily mutual prayer. The requests were primarily for guidance, but also for whatever intentions the Holy Spirit put in our heart that day. We still had many differences about lifestyle, especially in regard to family commitments. It is, however, so much easier to work out issues while talking and listening to God. Someone told us that it's difficult to remain at odds with someone you pray for. It's even more so when you're praying with the other person.

One Bread, One Body had been such a momentous part of our faith journey that we knew it must be shared. I had distributed about one hundred copies at the men's retreat, and we began giving copies to each new member of the Bible study, plus other friends and, of course, family members. We usually carry a small supply of books when we travel, to aid in evangelization. Our policy was to give only one copy to an individual. After that, it was up to them to request future issues. It was disappointing to see how few active Catholics took the next step on their own.

To reach more people, we decided to set up a booth at the next SCRC convention in Anaheim. Father Al graciously agreed to send all the literature if we would cover the fees. The big question was: how many copies of OBOB to request. We turned to our daily discernment prayer and settled on 500, even though there would be about twelve thousand attendees. When they turned out the lights in the exhibit hall on the last day, we had handed out 497 copies. God-incidence?

SPAN

It was about this time that Valerie was moved to share her journey in a very special way. For the years following her breast cancer, she worked as a volunteer in the American Cancer Society's outreach program. This involved visiting and trying to bring comfort to recently diagnosed women or those who were going through treatment. It is often said that the chemotherapy for cancer can be more devastating than the disease. With her natural physical and spiritual beauty, Valerie was ideal for the role and a true blessing to those she visited. The only downside was that ACS guidelines did not encourage the sharing of religious beliefs. This became a more serious issue as Valerie, like me, grew exponentially in her faith. The solution came when she formed a Christian cancer support group primarily for women.

Along with a small number of cancer survivors, they began bi-monthly meetings at our house for prayer and sharing. Other than being a woman, they began with recently diagnosed and going through treatment as a requirement. The one exception is my wife, the leader, who has been free of the disease for over 15 years. Eventually they named the group SPAN, short for St. Peregrine's Angels Network, after the patron saint for those who suffer from cancer. Another of those God-incidences occurred when they learned of a shrine to the saint at the San Juan Capistrano Mission, a short 30 miles north of Vista.

Twenty or more women have wandered through the network's meetings, along with an occasional man allowed in to be prayed over. It would be wonderful to report numerous miracles, but the truth is that for almost every recovery or remission, there has been a non-survivor. But even those whom God chose to call have shared their final moments with more love and compassion than could be available in our secular society, because it's God's love they are sharing. I have gotten to know most of the women, plus husbands and family members. It's clear that we can all handle the extreme grief of loss through the grace and strength of God and the support of other believers.

SPAN has recently been recognized by Father Ramon, our pastor, as an official ministry of St. Francis of Assisi parish. The organization is now publicized as a Christian cancer support group for women offering:

Support
Prayer
Among us, Christ is present
Never lose hope in God's healing power

Let us close with "A Prayer to St. Peregrine for One Suffering from Cancer":

Dear St. Peregrine,
I need your help.
I feel so uncertain
of my life right now.
This serious illness makes me long for
a sign of God's love.
Help me to imitate your enduring faith
when you faced the ugliness
of cancer and surgery.
Allow me to trust the Lord
the way you did in
this moment of distress.
I want to be cured,
but right now I ask God for
the strength to bear the cross in my life.
I seek the power to proclaim
God's presence in my life
despite the hardship, anguish and fear
I now experience.
O glorious St. Peregrine,
be an inspiration to me
and petitioner of these needed graces
from our loving Father.
Amen

The Year of God the Father

Although the year of The Holy Spirit had been a period of phenomenal spiritual growth, we were still searching for God's calling. Reflecting on the words of Jesus like, *"for he who has much, much is expected"* and *"you will do greater things then Me,"* it was obvious that our blessings demanded we play a much bigger role in the Kingdom of God on earth. So we continued asking for guidance, especially during the periodic pilgrimages.

With ministries, children, grandchildren and aging parents, we no longer had the luxury of marathon trips. Our plans for this spring revolved around visiting the only seven states we had missed in 1992, all in the Northwest. In preparation, we had purchased a half dozen Christian travel guides like:

Liguori Guide to Catholic USA
A Place for God
Marian Shrines of the United States

Details on these and others may be found in the Appendix. The beauty of RV travel is the flexibility to change plans at the last minute. I'm not egotistical enough to think that God gave our destination states an extra dose of winter so we would change our route, but that is what happened. At the last minute we settled on a slow-paced journey throughout California, something we had never done before. In the three years preceding the jubilee, people all over the world were planning pilgrimages to holy places, and so we followed suit. What better place than our own home state, filled with missions, large and small churches, plus hundreds of places named after saints. Starting with San Diego, we wandered north along the coast, following the path of Father Junipero Serra if he had been driving a 30-foot motor home.

I've often thought of compiling a travel book devoted to religious sites throughout the United States, but that's not what this is all about. We are on a much more rewarding journey and so will dispense with travelogue-type details. Again, because we were still searching, our frequent prayers continued to ask God for direction. In a relatively short time, He made it abundantly clear that we were heading away from the destination chosen for us, Vista. As mentioned previously, Vista has a population of about 84,000. For many that's a big city, but by California standards it's a small town. Also, it's not a particularly affluent community, not filled with frequent flyers, but at almost every stopover we encountered other travelers who either called Vista home or had relatives and friends living there. Contemplate for a moment the odds of two or more people from the same small piece of real estate, on this vast earth, ending up at the same time in another remote location. Now consider the odds of this occurring over and over again.

As mentioned, we have painted on the back of our RV in six-inch high letters, "LET US PRAY." Also a bumper sticker reads:

> The Holy Spirit Is Alive
> at St. Francis of Assisi
> Catholic Church
> Vista, California

It was amazing how few acknowledged these witness statements. However, those that did seemed appreciative of our outreach and provided confirmation of God's message. The first occurred in Pfieffer State Park, near Big Sur. A woman parked directly across the road informed us that she had lived in Vista and actually attended our church. Coincidence??? Maybe, but only 20 feet away?

While spending a few days in the redwoods, we found ourselves surrounded by a group of young Christian families tent camping together. One couple, noticing our bumper sticker, relayed that they had relatives living in Vista, one of whom was on the city council. They were just returning from a family visit there. Before parting we all joined hands and praised God, surrounded by some of His most majestic creations. The young people referred to us as evangelical Catholics. We liked that.

By this time, God was hoping we had received the message, but just in case, He saw fit to use the old mallet-to-the-head approach, reserved for the childlike. The setting was truly a small town, Ferndale, population 1300, located just southwest of Eureka. The entire city center is designated a state historical landmark. So scenic is the downtown that it has been reproduced in Legos as the only United States small community represented in Legoland. With all this recognition it draws a fair share of tourists, particularly on this July 4th weekend. The highlight of the festivities was the annual patriotic parade. The town is so small and participants so few that they actually run the parade up and down main street twice.

Thinking they might repeat a third time, we elected to wander onto a beautiful setting at the far end of the business district. It turned out to be the site of an old and immaculately maintained cemetery, complete with flowers, massive headstones and shrines to former Ferndale residents. It was quite a steep climb to the top level, but well worth it. From the highest peak you could see all the activities in this picturesque hamlet.

For a while we were the only two taking advantage of this setting. As we began our decent, another couple came into view. Much to our surprise, the man was wearing a shiny red satin-like jacket embroidered on the left front with "St. Francis of Assisi." Valerie was quick to point out that there are hundreds, maybe thousands of schools and churches named after St. Francis. After all, it is one of the largest orders in the world. It didn't matter. My curiosity had to be satisfied.

Approaching them I said, "Where we come from, at the Friday morning Mass we often sit behind groups of children wearing the same type of jacket."

To which he replied, "I'm sure it's not the same place; this jacket comes from a small, faraway town of Vista." The other Joe had been a music director and his wife Liz a second grade teacher at – you guessed it – St. Francis of Assisi Catholic Church, Vista, California. The mallet left a knot on both our heads that never went away.

So we headed south, back to where God was calling our ministry. The message was clear, and possibly it should have been time for God to rest in the knowledge that "we got it," but He didn't. We proceeded down the much faster but less scenic route I-5, singing and praising The One now in complete control of our journey.

Well, almost. With a few days to spare, we decided to complete the trip with one last stop, at one of our favorite meccas on the coast. To do so, we headed west, just north of Los Angeles, over the hills back to the coastal highway where we turned north. If the windows were not up and praise music not blaring, we might have heard a deep, booming voice from the clouds yelling, " STOP!!!, TURN AROUND, I SAID 'SOUTH TO VISTA'."

But we didn't hear, so this time He brought out the bigger iron mallet, in the shape of a large travel bus. From seemingly out of nowhere, this oversized vehicle sped up on our left side and then maneuvered a dangerously close swerve into our lane, almost forcing us off the freeway. Before screaming, we were forced to acknowledge God's presence as we saw the back of the bus. There in foot-high, black letters against a white background was the one word:

VISTA

The bus exited the next off ramp, which had the familiar name of "Vista del Mar," exactly the same as that of the senior community we call home.

Our friend Father Al used to say, "Sometimes God just wants to be God." Our prayer after settling our nerves was, "Yes, Lord, we understand, Vista, but we are just taking a couple of days rest." He allowed us to continue north a few miles, to Carpinteria State Beach. While we were jockeying the RV in to a seaside parking space, the woman next to us took a look at the back end of our rig and said, "We have a son that lives in –"

I abruptly interrupted with, "Yes, yes, we know – Vista."

Jubilee

Here we were in the year of the pilgrimage with instructions from the Holy Spirit to remain in Vista for our ministry. Even Pope John Paul II was offering a plenary indulgence as part of the travel package. It went something like this:

> Step 1 – Visit a site designated by the Pope, or a local Bishop, as a Jubilee destination.
>
> Step 2 – Participate in the sacrament of Reconciliation and the Eucharist.
>
> Step 3 – Recite certain prayers for the intentions of the Pope.
>
> Step 4 – Ask God for the indulgence to be applied for someone that had already died, or for yourself. Offering the prayers for some other living human being apparently didn't work.

The resultant blessing was freedom from purgatory for the dead person or expiation of all temporal punishment due for your own sins, up to that date. You could not clear the slate for the entire balance of your life.

With these miraculous carrots dangling before us, we still remained faithful to the calling. For most of the year our efforts concentrated on Bible study, homeless shelter, and SPAN and a few local retreats. But after attending a talk on pilgrimages, our wanderlust took over and we struck a compromise, maybe one sided but a compromise nonetheless.

While others were traveling to Rome, Jerusalem and Assisi, we made our plans for a holy journey through San Diego County. Bishop Brom had designated five historical missions as Jubilee sites. Over the next five weeks, we traveled to four of them. Starting at Mission San Luis Rey a short 20 minutes from home, we parked our RV in the back lot. At the end of a weekend retreat for married couples, Father Bill prepared to celebrate Mass in the old mission church. He reminded all present that this was one of the bishop's sites and that if we followed all the aforementioned steps, we could gain an indulgence for a deceased loved one or ourselves.

This was to be my first and greatest test of faith in the Pope's promise. The designated recipient for the benefits of my prayers was Julia Amelia Stevens, my mother. The big concern was not getting her out of purgatory, but whether or not she had been blessed with

His Plan -- My Conversion

that temporary holding place. Mom had a particularly difficult life, beginning as a Polish migrant worker in the fields and canneries along the Eastern Seaboard. Apparently this is the way her parents made a living with their six or so children, none of whom got to school. As an adult she suffered frequent physical and emotional illnesses which put her in various hospitals, 23 at last count. The final devastation was spinal surgery that left her paralyzed from the waist down. At age 57, one day after holding our newborn daughter for the first time, she took her own life. Teachings of the Catholic church at that time were that suicide resulted in an immediate sentence to the fires of hell. I had my doubts, but with my childlike beliefs, for this one I was going to need a sign, a big sign.

Just prior to Mass Father Bill asked if I would do the readings, of course. It was one of those unusual liturgies when two alternate passages were offered for the first reading. He left the decision in my hands. Not having time to peruse the possibilities in advance, I blindly selected Song of Songs, chapter 3, verses 1-4. The final lines brought joy to my heart, as I read:

I found him whom my heart loves.
I took hold of him and would not let go of him
till I should bring him to
the home of my mother.

Once again, The Lord has chosen Scripture to give me a sign, a very big sign.

With such a powerful start to the journey, we were prepared for anything except disappointment. The next stop, about 40 miles down a winding road, was Mission San Antonio De Pala, a small and very beautiful Indian place of worship. The grounds and surrounding area had been laid out, many years ago, with horses and wagons in mind, not 30-foot class A motor homes. There was just no place to park, and so we moved on. Disappointment should not have entered our thoughts, considering who was really in charge of this pilgrimage. We would in later months and years return to the little Indian mission many times for Sunday Mass.

The next prayer offering was for my father, John Joseph Szczepanski. While in the third grade, my parents legally changed our name to Stevens. Much later, I learned this was actually a literal translation from the Polish, meaning "son of or belonging to Stevens," or more commonly, "Stevenson." With the miracle of my mother's transition fresh in my mind, I was not requesting another sign. My faith was restored, but we already know God doesn't trust me with only one miraculous revelation.

We entered Santa Ysabel Mission just before Mass. While reciting the obligatory indulgence prayers for my dad, I glanced to the left at the reconciliation room. There above the center door was the pastor's name, William Stevenson (translates into Polish as

Szczepanski). After Mass I went to the sacristy and shared the God-incidence with pastor Bill. He was pleased, but not the least bit surprised.

The fourth church on our holy trek was San Diego de Acala, the first of Father Junipero Serra's missions. This time the prayers would be for Ange, sister and mentor. If not for her, at age 18 I might have purchased the new Ford Fairlane convertible and never started college. Unfortunately, she, like the rest of my family, died at a relatively early age and never got to share in my conversion, although after this trip, they would all be looking down on us. The Mass was uneventful and exactly what a Catholic expects, until just before the end.

The Holy Spirit recognized the special place Ange has in my heart, so She sent in the first string. Phoebe flew through an open window and settled on a rafter just over our heads and remained till the final dismissal. To make sure that I got the blessing, she flew across our path as we exited the church.

Phoebe's appearance punctuated the indulgence services for my sister Bernie and brother-in-law, Jim. Actually, the only non-confirmation came when I prayed for myself. God does have a sense of humor, I hope!!! If you're keeping score at home, I've mentioned four locations and six indulgences. It was acceptable to return to a designated holy place and repeat the procedure for a different person. The fifth site offered by Bishop Brom was St. Thomas Indian Mission at Fort

Yuma. This one is actually out of San Diego County, and our Travel Agent may have chosen to send a big bus after us again.

Since this is my book, I only shared my personal miracles. Valerie was also blessed in response to prayers for her first husband Ken, father-in-law Alex, and her Aunt Fran. My wife has greater faith than I and does not ask for signs.

In addition to the spirituality of these sojourns, there was a practical lesson to be learned. This relatively short trip of many stops was limited by the somewhat cumbersome 30-foot motor home. The failed visit at Pala was only one of several aborted stops due to a no-room-at-the-inn parking lot. We began to consider alternatives, like a truck trailer combination. Obviously, after parking a trailer, you have the mobility of a smaller vehicle. One major benefit is the flexibility for weekday Mass like we have at home. We were, however, hesitant about being frivolous with the financial blessings God provided.

Although we are not wealthy, God has graciously allowed adequate resources. In little ways we try to share our comfort. In addition to tithing and instead of garage sales, portions of our abundance go to Catholic Charities. So the response to our daily prayers of discernment probably should not have come as a surprise, but it did.

The word I received first was to donate the motor home prior to purchasing something new. Being raised

His Plan -- My Conversion

in a poor family, the idea of giving away about $17,000 (Blue Book value) did not come easily. Surely Valerie, being more frugal, would object, but she agreed with a joyful heart. The more we talked and prayed, the more obvious God's will became.

The only difference of opinion was that I wanted to take the easy way out and give the RV to Father Joe, who ran the San Diego homeless shelters and advertised they would do all the paperwork and pick up the vehicle. Valerie, on the other hand, wanted to sell and split the proceeds amongst several charities. God again stepped in.

Our farewell to the class A was a 200-mile drive north for the annual Thanksgiving Day family feast on the beach at Carpinteria. At about the 150-mile mark, the engine quit, never to run, <u>for us</u>, again. After towing, I told the garage owner about our charitable plans, hoping for a sympathetic quote for repair. Instead, he offered to buy the rig, as is, for $12,000. Although much lower than we hoped for, we accepted the offer. At least Valerie could now donate to the charities of her choice.

We returned home, cash in hand. Valerie looked through the Southern Cross Catholic newspaper for Father Joe's address and found he was running a large ad. Apparently, a major San Diego business firm had offered to match any donations to Father Joe for a limited time.

And so the proceeds from the sale of our motor home went like this:

Birth Choice	$3,000.00
Presentation Ministries (Father Al)	4,000.00
Father Joe	5000.00
Matching donation to Father Joe	5000.00
Total Proceeds to Charity	$17,000.00
	(Blue Book value)

God-incidence???

We headed into the new millennium with a truck, fifth wheel and a small library of books on "Holy Places to Visit in the United States."

What Now, Lord?

After the marvels of the Jubilee year, it appeared that 2001 would proceed at a much slower pace. Perhaps God was allowing rest prior to the challenges of 2002. Since the world did not end in 2000, the Little Rock Scripture Study lost many of those who joined only to study "Revelation." We settled back to an average of 120 members. Here again, 2002 held great promise as we prepared to continue the advanced studies while starting over for those with just a beginning interest in the Word of God.

Between SPAN and LRSS, we found time for little side trips, primarily to the solace of some beachfront campground. It was just one of those five-day jaunts to the Silver Strand State Beach in Coronado that put us in touch with another of God's minor miracles. We had taken the bus into downtown San Diego for the noon Mass at the Cathedral. I was wearing a bolo tie, completed earlier that morning using a miniature, wooden copy of the San Damiano Crucifix. The large versions of this multicolored icon hang above the altar in most Franciscan churches. You can read more about it in most biographies of St. Francis.

The bus had dropped us off about a half mile from St. Joseph's Cathedral. We slowly walked the inner city streets, passing a Christian church that had just finished serving breakfast to the homeless of the area. We arrived at our destination to find the Mass schedule had changed, and there would be another hour to wait. It never ceases to amaze me what God goes through to get people together at the right place and time.

Walking around waiting for the church to open, we again passed the previous breakfast site. There were several small groups of men just hanging around, maybe talking of better times. We exchanged shallow good mornings as people are apt to do when they are not completely comfortable.

Suddenly, one young unshaven fellow shouted, "I like your cross. I used to have one."

For some reason the thought went through my mind that he probably wasn't Catholic and probably did not appreciate the significance of this historic icon. He may have had a plain cross or a simple crucifix, but not like mine. Besides, it was an original that I had just created this morning. I said thank you and walked on.

After a few steps Valerie stopped me and said, "You should give it to him." I was shocked. My personal work of art??? Had she forgotten how long we searched for just the right size cross? But alas, she was right. We returned to the group of men and I handed the fellow my treasure, saying, "I'd like you to have this."

Now he was shocked and filled with joy. Tears came to his eyes, and mine. He said something like, "No one has ever done anything like this for me." We all chatted for a few minutes and exchanged names as we prepared to leave. My new friend was the last to take our hands and reveal, "My name is Francis."

Somewhere I read: *"be kind to those who come in to your life, you never know when you might be entertaining angels, or even greater"* (see Genesis 18:1-15).

The less than good news of 2001 came when my in-laws, Harvey and Mary, announced they were ready to move from Camarillo, 150 miles north, to Vista. Valerie and I had discussed this possibility, so she was prepared when her dad asked if there were any homes for sale in our community. The concerned daughter quickly told them that living that close was not a good idea. But in a nervous moment she blurted out, "But there are some really nice homes right around the corner." My already high blood pressure went up another 10 or 20 points.

It's time to confess the major flaw in my rapidly expanding Christian character. After six years on the path to conversion, I had learned to love all the new family members that came as part of the marriage package. Liking and enjoying them all the time had its limits, however. I became particularly agitated in direct proportion to the frequency of visits, especially if unannounced, in large numbers and in our small retirement home. This attitude should have come as no surprise to Valerie, since it had been included in my lengthy, pre-nuptial dissertation, "Everything You Need to Know About Joe." The subject had also been discussed with her sons, Doug and Greg. Debbie was living in Las Vegas at the time. All I could see, with Harvey and Mary less than a mile away, was lots and lots of family gatherings.

Probably my outlook came from living 15 years as a lonely alcoholic. Whatever the reason, I was no longer pleased with these feelings and prayed daily for the gift of unconditional love. I knew that moving to the San Diego area was the right thing for the aging couple. They needed the comfort of having family nearby. And besides, Harvey's driving, which had always been bad, was deteriorating rapidly.

All I ever wanted was a little space, like maybe 10 miles, and that, in my typical show of complete honesty, is what I told them. I was not prepared for the anger from Harvey and the hurt response from Mary, especially since she is also not much for gatherings. Although they disagreed, they seemed to accept my sincerity and postponed any action. After the dust settled, our relationship was intact and we continued our 150-mile long visits, at least for a while.

As I sat and prayed, Phoebe stopped by again. Just briefly she sat on her usual spot atop the fence and then quickly disappeared. I prayed she would not give up on me.

I have been trying to get a picture, of the winged Paraclete, but so far have been unsuccessful. A couple of times she sat long enough for me to focus and shoot, but when the film was developed, our feathered advocate was either a blur or non-existent. In our travels we encountered certain Indian tribes who would not allow photographs because they believed it took away their spirit.

This brings us to our next and certainly one of the holiest pilgrimages. It may seem that frequent and extensive travel is not appropriate for ones trying to follow the teachings and example of Jesus. We continue to pray and discern about the use of our blessings, and it was during this trip that we received some insight into our luxury. Everything we have is a gift from God – not just our spouse, children and grandchildren, but also our home and car and even our RV. All gifts are to be used as He intended and then given back or passed on to His next designated beneficiary. Above all, our gifts must be used in such a way as to always praise God.

Our Father deserving of praise was never more apparent than at the Canyon de Chelly in Northeast Arizona. Recently a friend used the term "the church of the great outdoors," a very appropriate description for this lesser known of God's creations. Besides the unparalleled beauty, we also learned how the Indians used this gift to sustain and protect their families. There are sites like this all over the world, unspoiled by excessive human intervention, that now exist primarily to reflect the wonder and glory of their Maker.

As with other recent journeys, we referred to our small library of spiritual destinations for guidance. Nowhere is there a greater abundance of places to worship then in Arizona and New Mexico. As mentioned, this is not a travel guide, but there are a couple of holy places that must be recommended.

One of the most beautiful, that will not be found in any of the books, is in the small town of Chinle, just west of the Canyon de Chelly entrance. Our Lady of Fatima Church is built in the style of an Indian hogan. Although a fairly modern structure, the inside is finished with materials available to even the earliest inhabitants. In addition to the rich woods, the church is decorated with living plants and animal skins that rival the finest art exhibits. The pastor of any cathedral would be proud to have the exquisite altar chair covered in brown and white cowhide. Even though the church was empty, you could feel the presence of The Great Spirit and His people.

Another highlight came at the Sanctuario de Chimayo about forty miles north of Santa Fe, New Mexico. Unlike the previous house of worship, this remote Spanish chapel is mentioned in almost every Christian guidebook and is often called "The Lourdes of America." Briefly, the miracle story is that a Don

His Plan -- My Conversion

Bernado Abeyta, after praying and recovering from a serious illness, had a vision to dig in a certain spot. There he found a crucifix, and there he built a chapel. The exact location, where the crucifix was found, is maintained in a small room, directly behind the altar. Like the other visitors we knelt and filled our plastic bags with "Holy Dirt" from the original hole, to share with our friends back home. This area, along with an adjacent, much larger room, is filled with crutches, braces and other mementos from those who have experienced a miraculous healing. Obviously, with hundreds of visitors filling their bags, the hole should have been much larger, but we were told the earth is replenished with loose soil from around the grounds every day by a worker, for the entire area is considered "Holy." This revelation is substantiated by the sign on the restaurant and gift shop across the road, offering for sale "Holy Chilies."

Briefly, let's return to the subject of discerning in the material world. Father Al in his book "Seek the Gifts of the Spirit" lists discernment of spirits as a charism. He goes on to say that there are three different spirits: The Holy Spirit, evil spirit, and our own human spirit. The secret is to know which is guiding our life at any particular moment. Without the Holy Spirit we can easily be deceived. Are we rationalizing about the RV and travel? Maybe, but after years of prayer and meditation, I feel at peace, God continues to guide and protect, and Phoebe continues to appear.

Year of the Not So Holy Family

It may not be obvious, but I really do want to relate better to the family that God has given me. I pray daily to love them all, unconditionally. This, most people would consider an integral part of a holy life, but for me it is still a struggle. Perhaps it is my cross.

In 2002 the Lord put me to the test. Not really meaning to hurt anyone, I had sent Harvey and Mary a letter explaining how we really wanted them in San Diego and that I was only asking for a little space. Taking this as an apology, they immediately put their house up for sale and purchased one around the corner – a mere 5,280 feet from ours, but who's counting. I was going to need extraordinary grace.

The blessing came in the form of a homily from our pastor, Father Ramon. Every year just before Lent, he gives the parishioners a message about sacrifice for the season. It stuck with me the first time I heard the message, the central theme being that whatever Lenten sacrifice you make, if it is truly worthy, should be incorporated

His Plan -- My Conversion

into the rest of your life. That was it!!! I would make Harvey and Mary my sacrifice. For the next 40 days I would show my in-laws unconditional love.

My prayer and commitment were more fervent than ever, and God responded with an outpouring of grace like I had never experienced. Just as when He took away my addictions to cigarettes and alcohol, the Father took away the anxiety and hostility I had been feeling. Once again there was peace. It began when I told the new Vista residents that we were glad they moved. Their hearts must be exceptional for people in their 80s, for neither fainted away. For the next 40 days, we showed them around with a certain amount of enjoyment, introduced them to new people and places and, in general, just tried to make them welcome. I even spent several days on chores Harvey could no longer do on his own.

One unique feature of the Vista area is the proximity of two Catholic churches, about two miles apart. In a show of consideration, the in-laws elected to join St. Thomas Moore parish, a new and somewhat modern facility. After a couple of months, Harvey admitted they were less than happy at a church without kneelers. At this point, it was obvious my commitment would last beyond Lent, when, without hesitation, I invited them to join St. Francis of Assisi, and so they did. I think after six months we all feel comfortable in the community we call Vista. The whole experience adds emphasis to the belief that, *"with God all things are possible."*

Is That All There Is???

Not really. But it does bring us to the present moment, and my conversion may only be in the earliest stages.

In Latin there are two words for conversion: conversio and conversatio. The former indicates a once-in-a-lifetime turning toward God, while the latter is a totally new way of daily living. A good analogy might be the difference between a wedding and marriage. We cradle Catholics have a blessing and maybe a curse, being born into the faith. The curse is the belief that conversion is for non-Catholics. We even call them converts. Hopefully, the experiences shared in the first part of this book points up the fallacy of that thinking. Just as I am a recovering alcoholic, I also consider myself a recovering Catholic. As mentioned earlier, many of the guests on Marcus Grodi's TV show "The Journey Home" are coming back to Catholicism. My journey is forward, to the full richness of a loving relationship with Jesus Christ. Borrowing a phrase used by many of our Christian brethren, through Baptism in the Holy Spirit, I am truly a born again Catholic.

We are approaching September. Grandchildren are going back to school, the next Bible study is organized and we will be planning the next pilgrimage. For me it will be a time of meditation and reflection, asking God what more do we share. Charisms (Gifts of the Holy Spirit) are given to individuals only to be shared with community, and I have Charisms in abundance. Considering what the Spirit has done with a divorced Catholic alcoholic from a poor, uneducated Polish family, *what greater can He do for you* if you just ask and listen to His Word.

If You Wish To Be Perfect

(Matthew 19:21)

Part 2:

A Simple Conversion Guide for Catholics

Introduction

Last night God woke me at about 2:00 am. Oh, He didn't shake me or even talk in a deep, booming voice. The truth is, He didn't use a voice at all. Some people claim to hear God's voice, but I'm not that blessed. No, He just filled my mind with ideas about what must be included in the rest of this book. He simply caused me to be wide awake and know that these thoughts bombarding me were directly from Him. Now, God has blessed me abundantly, including the gift of peaceful and sound sleep, almost every day – or night actually – of my life. So when He deliberately woke me, it had to be very important. All of a sudden God filled my heart and mind with a flurry of ideas and then allowed me to slip back in to a deep slumber. Unlike many dreams that fade upon awakening, the next morning every word was there, vivid in my mind. So as quickly as possible I committed it all to paper.

He began by raising questions, for me and you, the reader, like: why try to change, why seek conversion?

Introduction

Most of us are quite happy as lukewarm Catholics. The teachings of the Church always seem to be in opposition to what we hear in the real world. Why expose myself to that conflict? Besides, I don't have time or the inclination to get more involved with the church. That takes a lot of commitment, doesn't it? I'm quite happy as a cradle Catholic. After all, it's the way I was raised – go to church every Sunday, even though the Mass is boring and a little too long; receive the Eucharist, even though it's not all that clear to me; and go to confession, or is it reconciliation. I think those group penance services satisfy that requirement, don't they?

After all, I'm as good as the next guy, and now we learn, maybe even better than some priests and bishops. Besides, Jesus died for all our sins, so I'll probably go to Heaven. That's really what it's all about; Heaven or hell, isn't it?

<u>No, it isn't.</u>

But before we look at what "it is," let me acknowledge that the reason these words, received in the middle of the night, were so clear and easy to recall is that they described the way my religious process worked before the conversion journey began.

Now, again, if it's not about Heaven or hell, what then? First, I make no claim about a sure path to Heaven, although I believe we could all get to hell if we put our minds to it. Someday it will be about those two drastically different destinations, but for now, let's put them aside and focus on living God's kingdom here on this earth, with all of our humanism. That's what Jesus did while He was a resident among us.

For some, life may seem like hell. For most of us it's probably more like purgatory, and that just might be what it is. But once you begin to build a relationship with the Father, Son and Holy Spirit, your worldly woes and burdens begin to make sense as you proceed on a journey toward what is promised. All that Jesus asks is that we take up our cross daily and follow. Lest we worry too much about that cross, be assured that for the past 8 or 9 years of my journey, once I started to pay attention, the rewards far exceeded any cross I've had to carry. And maybe – most encouraging – you will never carry that cross alone again.

If you chose not to begin the journey, I can only say you don't know what you're missing, here, now and in the future called eternity. For man, woman and child *cannot see what greatness God has in store.*

So let me invite you to travel a most wondrous road to salvation, full of potholes, detours and areas under construction, but leading to the one ultimate destination. I firmly believe the way to Heaven is to begin living it here on earth, for *"there is no condemnation for those who are in Christ Jesus"* (Romans 8:1).

We will break the trip down into nine short steps. Being an AA alumnus I'd prefer it to be 12 steps, but the Holy Spirit only gave me 9, and as previously mentioned, there are times when God just wants to be

Introduction

God. In each step we will share more details of my personal experience and the resultant implications. Part 1 – simply tells what happened. Part 2 – attempts to explain not just why it happened, but what I may have done to facilitate God's work in me. It also addresses what you can do to allow Him to work miracles of conversion in your life. So join in traveling along the same or similar byways, while looking for the marvelous signposts of your own conversion. The steps we will take are:

1. Believe
2. Pray
3. Listen
4. Plan
5. Gifts
6. Lifestyle
7. Love
8. The Cross
9. Conversion

We RV travelers know that "the journey is as important as the destination." Our heritage is not so much the final outcome, but rather the day-to-day privilege of having God present. Be not afraid of the journey; be not afraid of conversion.

Step 1 – Believe

This is possibly the easiest, for most of us, and yet the most important. You know by now about my blessing of a child-like belief system. As far back as grammar school and continuing into my early senior citizen years, I accepted what the church taught as gospel. So, what does it mean to be childlike? Simply stated, if a parent tells their child a fact that is at least reasonable, the child, if not a teenager, will accept it on face value, just because it came from a parent that loves them and would not intentionally hurt them. It's the same with God. He is our Father, who loves us unconditionally and wants us to know the Truth. Certainly He wishes not to harm us but protects us from all evil, even from the likes of satan, even from our own self destructive tendencies called sin. After all, He sent His only Son to save us (John 3:16).

So what must we believe? For starters, <u>the Bible, Scripture, the Word of God</u>, and all three are the same. Now that should be easy. We already know that the

Step 1 – Believe

Bible is the inspired word of God. Some of it may be more difficult to understand than to believe, but that will be discussed later in the section on "Listening."

One of the most difficult truths to believe for many Catholics and most other Christians is the Eucharist: the fact that at Mass, bread and wine become the Body and Blood, Soul and Divinity of our Lord Jesus Christ. But this we must believe. It is paramount to our faith and sets us apart from most other Christian denominations. Why is it so difficult, when Jesus, in His own Words, gave us this miracle at the last supper and on the cross. He then went on to say: *"we should do this in memory of Him."* If you have difficulty with total belief, repeat the following passage: *"I do believe, help my unbelief."*

I'm reminded of a small part in a classic old movie, Stalag 17. After years in a German prisoner of war camp, a young American soldier receives a letter from his wife. In it she says, "You won't believe this, but someone left a baby on our doorstep, and you won't believe this, but the baby looks just like me." For the rest of the movie we see the soldier, sitting on his bunk, letter in hand repeating, "I believe it, I believe it." The more often we believe with our minds and our lips, the faster and more completely we will believe with our hearts.

Near the end for each of the steps I will quote the Scripture passages that most dramatically touched my heart. For each topic, you are encouraged to search the Bible for the Words of God that speak to you.

<u>God tells us to "Believe"</u>

The Gospel According to Mark:

(Mark 1:15): *Repent and believe in the gospel.*

(Mark 16:14): *Whoever believes and is baptized will be saved: whoever does not believe will be condemned.*

The Second Letter to Timothy

(2 Timothy 3:15-16): *Sacred Scriptures are capable of giving you wisdom for salvation -- All Scripture is inspired by God.*

The Letter to the Hebrews

(Hebrews 11:6): *anyone who approaches God must believe that He exists and that He rewards those who seek Him.*

The First Letter of Peter

(1 Peter 1:8): *Although you have not seen Him you love Him; even though you do not see Him now yet believe in Him, you rejoice.*

The word "believe" is used four times from verse 29 through 47 in John, chapter 6. Jesus teaches that we must believe in Him and in the truths He is revealing.

Step 2 – Pray

St. Isadore wrote: "When we pray we talk to God, when we read Scripture God talks to us." Now, I don't know anything about St. Isadore, other than he was a farmer, but that should not stop us from adopting his famous teaching. Did I mention that I also believe just about everything credited to a saint? It's possible that Scripture (listening to God) should have been addressed prior to prayer. After all, what God says must be more important than what we say. But that's not how it works for most of us, and certainly not for me. It wasn't clear what He was saying until after I began to pray "The Novena to the Holy Spirit," and the more I repeated that prayer, the clearer became God's Word for me, not just in Scripture, but in other holy writings, homilies, talks, etc. We were always taught in Catholic school to "avoid the near occasions of sin." It should then follow, the benefits of putting ourselves in the near occasion of God's grace, and prayer certainly puts us in His presence.

Valerie and I have participated in numerous forms of prayer, such as the 40-day retreat at Presentation Ministries, the annual SCRC convention, pilgrimages, Eucharistic adoration and frequent prayer breakfasts, lunches, dinners and even snacks. With all the churches in Vista and the surrounding area, there is no shortage of opportunities for acts of devotion. As our faith grew so did our participation. A day does not pass that we do not put ourselves in that blessed near occasion.

Prayer did not come easily at first, and, actually, at times it still doesn't, but hopefully practice will make perfect. One reason it is so difficult to pray is the overwhelming wonder as to how anything we think of to say can bear any significance to the omnipotent presence we call Our Father. However it's not like that. He is interested in our every thought and every word, so much that He provides the Holy Spirit to lift our prayers.

I recall one day, while parked at the Silver Strand beach in Coronado. Looking at the beauty and wonder of the ocean and sky, with the rolling, crashing waves washing the beach, it occurred that I can't possibly thank and praise the Father adequately, or even close for the majesty and wonder of His creation. Then I noticed a picture of Jesus and Mary and again realized that I can't praise or thank Jesus enough for dying on the cross for my sins. I can't, in human word or thought, acknowledge Mary's role in salvation history. And that is why *the Holy Spirit must take over our meager*

Step 2 – Pray

offerings and make them suitable, even pleasing to God.

So we just pray as best we can.

Let me address the problems encountered when first I felt the need for more fervor in my prayer life. As a cradle Catholic, having four years of grammar school at Sacred Heart, I learned to pray every day, mainly just before bedtime. Like the rest of my faith status, the prayers were repetitious and very shallow. But the more I called upon the Holy Spirit, the more my prayer and understanding matured. It was, however, as recent as two months ago that I discovered a new prayer method that overtook my nightly petitions. It truly is an ongoing, ever-growing process.

The first question some may ask is, why pray. After all, does the Bible not say that *God knows what we need, even before we ask*. My best answer comes from Father Jim Nisbet, a Bible scholar who teaches: "We are not only called to do what Jesus tells us, but also to do as Jesus did, to imitate His holy life, and Jesus did pray, to the Father, often."

Later we will examine Jesus and His prayers, for He shows us not only how, when and where, but even provides the words. In preparing for this book, I came across a note in my 1997 journal:

"Why must I pray? What is the purpose of my prayers?

1. To praise, worship and express my love for God.

2. To seek forgiveness (redemption).

3. To ask for guidance.

4. For strength to do God's will.

It is enlightening to ask questions like this periodically and observe the changes in response that reflects our growth. That is the value of journaling.

The number one question in my beginning prayer life was to whom do we address these devotions. After all, there is God the Father, God the Son, and God the Holy Spirit. Do we pray to all three as the Trinity? This seemed awkward; the Trinity is difficult enough to comprehend, even without trying to communicate. Shall we speak with just one, like the Holy Spirit, and as we noted, let Him (or Her) carry our message on high. Father Tom Allendar, a brilliant retreat master, once told us that he prays exclusively to the Father, while others suggest that Jesus is the only one that became human and therefore may be better suited to carry our message. The answer is simple: I don't know. After years of struggle my prayer technique has evolved and can best be explained by my personal Sign of the Cross: "I pray to you, Father, in the name of Your Son, Jesus Christ, with the help and guidance of Your Holy Spirit." In time, it will become very personal to you, also.

Step 2 – Pray

Another entry from my 1999 journal addresses the subject this way: "It's okay to speak directly to God the Father and to Jesus and to the Holy Spirit individually or together. They will all hear you."

Almost everyone who has written or spoken on the subject agrees on certain aspects of prayer: It's important to give God our best, in time, place and everything else, for that matter. As mentioned in Part 1, being a morning person, most of my meditation and reading is accomplished even before the first cup of coffee, and some even before my feet first touch the floor. Valerie, on the other hand, can't communicate with me, much less God, before the caffeine kicks in, but she talks to God throughout the day, kind of like Tevya in Fiddler on the Roof. Also, before bedtime, she has some ritualistic prayers to complete. Our differences still cause difficulty in establishing a time for joint prayer, and yet this mutual offering may be the most significant, since two are gathered, in His name, for the same purpose, primarily praising and asking for guidance as a couple whom God made one.

The gap between morning and evening prayers more and more is being filled in, like Valerie, with continuous spiritual comments on just about everything occurring throughout the day. Sometimes I feel a need to apologize for being too trivial in the subject matter. Finally, near bedtime, I sit in the prayer chair or kneel before a Crucifix for a combination of semi-meditation, old-time simple prayers and trying to listen. This is the most difficult, being basically brain dead after 9:00 p.m. I tend to believe that God accepts and is pleased with any time we devote to Him, I hope.

The instructions from most who seem to know is to set aside a specific time and quiet place to pray each day. Of course, there is a lot to be said for speaking to God at every opportunity; such as when stuck in traffic, waiting in line or at a doctors office, or just waiting, period. We Americans do a lot of that and impatiently, I might add. So why not ask God for a dose of patience.

So far we have just looked at personal prayer, but as Valerie and I grew, so did the opportunities and types of prayer. Let me briefly address, with a little detail, the other variations mentioned at the beginning of this section. The easiest way is to outline what have been the sustaining elements of our spiritual journey.

Mass is probably the most significant form of prayer in our lives. First, of course, it is a celebration of the Body and Blood of our Lord Jesus Christ. He is present to us, and we are in His presence. Also, in the "Liturgy of the Word," we are given the opportunity to participate in the reading of Scripture, preparing us for His coming in the Eucharist. But even before all that glory, we enter the church and begin with personal prayers and intentions, followed by the greetings in word and song from this gathered community of faith, all as one, in the same purpose, to give God our praise, worship and love. After Scripture we are blessed with

Step 2 – Pray

the homily, an explanation and exhortation for this assembled Body of Christ, based on the Word we have just received. Listen intently and try to put the celebrant's declaration into the context of your present day. Often we find a message, prophecy, if you will, addressing immediate needs, concerns or questions. There have been homilies where the only thing missing was that the priest didn't start by calling my name.

If the Bible is a library of books, then the Mass is a medley of devotion, encompassing personal, family, community, Scriptural, intercessory, petition, praise, worship and even fasting, in preparation for the Eucharist. Speaking of medley, most parishes are blessed with music ministries that add a whole new dimension to prayer. It has been said that when we sing, we pray twice. Be not ashamed to sing, for as our own Sister. Madeline says: "God gave you a voice, so give it back to Him." When now I realize what is included in a Mass, it's incomprehensible that it ever seemed boring. I just didn't get it.

Someday we pray to follow Father Al's exhortation for daily Mass, but for now, we try not to let two days pass without celebrating Mass. If you are currently a "go-to-church-on-Sunday Catholic," let me offer a suggestion, Try going one additional day during the week when it's not a special occasion. Just go to Mass for the sake of going to Mass. If scheduling is a problem, check the directory for your diocese. These books are usually available in your parish office or at a

Catholic bookstore. We have found numerous evening and afternoon Masses within a 10-mile radius. If you still can't find a suitable time, try sitting with Jesus for an hour in an adoration chapel and let His love wash over you. Then just think – you are in the presence of our Lord and Savior, Jesus Christ.

WOW!!!

Retreats, one of our favorite prayer forms, come in many shapes and sizes, from the monthly, three-hour (including Mass and dinner) twilight retreat, such as given at the Mission San Luis Rey in Oceanside, California, to the 40 days of small Christian community living offered by Presentation Ministries in Peebles, Ohio. They are equally as variant in size and tone – from the Labor Day weekend SCRC gathering of 12,000 charismatics, to days of utter silence for individuals or small groups at numerous monasteries throughout the country. There are retreats for almost every type of people, satisfying a multitude of needs such as: singles, married, engaged, alcoholics, homosexuals, overeaters and just about every other addiction, illness or lifestyle.

In the Appendix you will find a small list of books providing a selection of retreat houses. It's a perfect way for a relatively inexpensive vacation to renew body, soul and relationship. At St. Francis of Assisi Parish, twice a year we have a guest retreat master for about

Step 2 – Pray

four days, providing what is typically called a mission, an at-home retreat. If this is not currently offered at your church, make it your evangelistic duty and benefit the entire community or investigate the possibilities at neighboring parishes.

During my career in Aerospace sales, each company represented would bring in all the sales people, typically twice a year, to be pumped up with enthusiasm and sent back in the field to do battle with our customers. Retreats are like that. We get pumped up with faith and love to evangelize and do battle with the bad guys. Valerie and I have attended about every type of retreat and mission. Never have we come away without a renewed enthusiasm for our faith journey.

We will look more at personal prayer in the section on listening to God (Scripture), but a most important form is encouraged by Jesus Himself when saying *if two, three or more are gathered in My name, I am there.* If we learn to pray as couples, families and small Christian communities, we reap the benefits of His presence. This is awkward for many, but remember, we have super spiritual support.

Simply start with, "Come, Holy Spirit," and then rest in His closeness; it will come naturally. Sometimes it's best to ask the Spirit, "For what shall we pray," then close your eyes and wait quietly for His prompting. If that doesn't work for you, at least you have experienced a brief period of peaceful meditation. It will all come with time.

Remember, don't fear silence, and let the Holy Spirit lead you.

Public prayer appears to be the most difficult for "Cradle Catholics." We began by making the Sign of the Cross and saying grace aloud in restaurants, even fast food places. This grew into openly thanking God in all kinds of gatherings, especially family. As we grew in faith, there was a corresponding increase in the opportunities for open, even the dreaded impromptu, prayer. Again, simply call upon the Holy Spirit and begin by thanking and praising God. Since He is the source of all things, you will never run out of blessings to acknowledge or reasons to praise. Just look around. Although Father Al would say, "When you get around to praising God as the 'Lion of Juda,' you have probably reached the end. By that time you will probably be ready for the gift of tongues."

The last and one of the most powerful forms of prayer to be considered is fasting. Never underestimate the power of offering sacrifice, and not just during Lent. Recall what our pastor, Father Ramon, reminds us every year, that what we offer God during lent should really be a lifelong, life-changing forfeiture.

Before we get into Scripture passages on prayer, let me share a few quotes and prayers gathered from various sources:

> Unless you pray, you will be a Godless theologian.

Step 2 – Pray

If you don't pray, you may be tempted to seek a "better" (?) life, not with God.

The most the world can teach is how to cheat well.

Pray to be healed. The Lord will heal, but maybe not your body.

God doesn't need your words; He wants your heart.

Pray to do God's will, by His standards.

Do you live your prayers, or merely say your prayers?

Pray for the ability to pray.

Special Prayers

Father, do in me what You must, in order to do through me what You will.

Father, may I not have anything You don't want me to have.

Jesus, may I trust enough to hear anything You say.

Jesus, may I live the life You died on the cross, for me to live.

Lord Jesus, Son of God, have mercy on me a sinner.

Remember, prayer alone is not sufficient. *"Not everyone who says to Me, Lord, Lord, will enter the kingdom of Heaven, but only the one who does the will of the Father."(Matthew 7:21)*

God tells us to pray:

"Go to your room, close the door, and pray to your Father, in secret" (Matthew 6:6).

"Love your enemies and pray for those who persecute you" (Matthew 5:44).

"Jesus went up on the mountain by Himself to pray" (Matthew 14:23).

"Whatever you ask for, in prayer with faith, you will receive" (Matthew 21:22).

"For we do not know how to pray as we ought, but the Spirit itself, intercedes" (Romans 8:26).

"Have no anxiety at all, but in everything, by prayer and petition, with thanksgiving, make your requests known to God" (Philippians 4:6).

Step 2 – Pray

In Matthew 6:9-15 Jesus tells us how to pray when He gives us "The Our Father," and in 16-18 He teaches about fasting.

Many scholars consider John, chapter 17, The Prayer of Jesus, the basis for all prayer. And finally, the simplest and most powerful instruction: *"Pray always"* (Luke 18:1).

Step 3 – Listen

There is a distinction between Scripture and listening to God. In reality, it's not so much with listening as with hearing God, and here there is a major difference. Since we believe that the Bible is the inspired Word of God, then when we read, in fact, we are listening to His Word. Understanding, however, how those words apply to us in the present moment is hearing and, for most, much more of a challenge. Many hear God even without opening the Bible. In Part 1 I told about the number of times He encouraged me to quit drinking, using radio commercials. He used, I believe, alternate methods because, at the time, I was not reading Scripture. You can probably identify ways that God communicates, but if not, don't worry; it will soon come.

Hearing what God has to say is the single most important element in a faith journey. If we don't hear, how can we possibly understand what He expects, what His plan is for us as individuals. It is when we learn

Step 3 – Listen

to hear God and understand our role in the salvation plan that life really becomes exciting. It is my opinion that the easiest way to hear God is through His Word, Scripture.

Before we delve into Scripture, I did promise to mention personal prayer, speaking to God, as it relates to listening. Let us look at how it works for me. As mentioned, each morning I call upon the Spirit for guidance in my life. After a period of praise and thanksgiving, I ask the Father, Son and Holy Spirit to strengthen me for whatever is expected of me that day. I then turn to the Bible for the daily readings, followed by the meditations from OBOB. If we go to daily Mass, the readings are repeated, with another commentary, in the homily. Frequently, from Scripture, commentary, or meditations, written or spoken, the Lord will provide a word of guidance for my life, usually one day at a time. The more we pray, the more we read, the more we believe and trust, the clearer we will hear. I'm sure that's why God exhorts us to *"Pray Always."*

There is a saying, attributed to St. Jerome, one of the foremost Catholic Scripture scholars and commentators on the Bible, "Ignorance of Scripture is ignorance of Jesus." When involved in study of the Word, we encounter that quote over and over to the point of minimizing its significance. If we don't experience the life and teaching of Jesus, God the Father and the Holy Spirit, how can we possibly understand? Yet, if we do make the effort to read and accept God's Word, then even the meaning of our life will be made clear. It all becomes really quite simple, because our Lord didn't intend for his lessons to be complex or baffling. He meant them for the childlike. So when Jesus thought they might be confusing, He put them into parables. It's our culture that twists the meaning and tries to make us believe that following Jesus is not that easy and rewarding. But those are the words of the antichrist, not our savior, who says: *"My burden is light and my yoke is easy."*

The Bible is the best selling book of all time because it is the most exciting book ever written. Every time you read Scripture, a different message is revealed, even if the readings are only days apart, because the message is specifically for you at that precise time in your life. You only have to listen. In our society, people spend billions of dollars on so-called "self help" books. If we could experience "self help," the book would not be required. The Bible offers true self help – we need only to open our hearts and He will provide all the help we will ever need, even in the most trying times.

In the Appendix, you will find a listing for Bibles, commentaries and other writings that should assist in the journey into Scripture.

For now, let me offer a few basics for getting started. Begin with the New Testament. Read the Bible slowly and accept all that it says as "Gospel." If a passage or word is unclear, move on. The more you read and study, the more you will understand. Highlight and annotate the passages speaking to you. Later, when you look back, those passages will reveal a pattern of personal growth. And try not to become overly academic in your studies. Knowledge is no substitute for faith.

In order to prepare the balance of this chapter, I reviewed the highlighted areas of my personal New American Bible, so that I might share those passages having an early and significant impact on my conversion path. This is by no means the whole of my notes from over seven years, but a small sampling to help you appreciate how God relates to an individual at a particular time. The listing bears no relationship to the chronology of my life. With exception of the first revelation, the order will somewhat follow the books of the New Testament. Certainly, not all books are included.

The Gospel According to John (John 6:66-68): *Many of His disciples returned to their former way of life and no longer accompanied Him. Jesus then said to the twelve, "do you want to leave?" Simon Peter answered Him, "Master, to whom shall we go?"* It became clear to me that there is no other place to turn, and so I must know what He teaches.

The Gospel According to Matthew (Matthew 5:3-10):

The Beatitudes

Blessed are the poor in spirit,

for theirs is the kingdom of heaven.

Blessed are they who mourn,

for they will be comforted.

Blessed are the meek,

for they will inherit the land.

Blessed are they who hunger and thirst for righteousness

for they will be satisfied.

Blessed are the merciful,

for they will be shown mercy.

Blessed are the clean of heart,

for they will see God.

Blessed are the peacemakers,

for they will be called children of God.

Blessed are they who are persecuted for the sake of

righteousness,

for theirs is the kingdom of heaven.

Most teachers consider these verses as instructions on how we are to live. Often they are equated in importance to the Ten Commandments. For me the list was difficult to understand, much less follow, until a talk by Father Jim Nisbet explained them as a call for greatness that we, as humans, cannot possibly achieve but for which we must always strive. Following is an interpretation by Father Al from OBOB:

Be *"poor in spirit."* By voluntary poverty, we downsize our lives and in some ways live below our means.

> Sorrowfully repent of our sins and to express this in Confession.
>
> Be lowly, humble, submissive, and docile.
>
> Want righteousness and holiness more than we want to breathe, eat, or drink.
>
> *Show mercy;* that is, to treat others better than they deserve.
>
> Be single-hearted; that is, to live for the Lord alone with a pure heart and not with mixed motives.
>
> Be peacemakers, even at the cost of our lives (see Colossians 1:20).
>
> Be persecuted for love of Jesus. This is the ultimate privilege.

(Matthew 5:37): *Let your "yes" mean "yes" and your "no" mean "no." Anything else is from the evil one.* One of my favorites, in support of complete honesty, also mentioned again in James.

(Matthew 9:17): *People do not put new wine into old wineskins. Otherwise the skins burst, the wine spills out, and the skins are ruined. Rather, they pour new wine into fresh wineskins, and both are preserved.*

One of the more difficult passages to interpret until we accept that we are being called to a complete change, giving our whole life to God – "Conversion."

(Matthew 10:5-6): *Do not go into pagan territory or enter a Samaritan town. Go rather to the lost sheep of the house of Israel.* Jesus was sent, and in turn, sent His disciples, not to everyone but only to "the chosen people." Later Paul was commissioned to offer salvation to us, the gentiles. We, in turn, must minister first to our Christian brothers and sisters.

(Matthew 11:25 and 18:3): *Father, although You have hidden these things from the wise, and the learned, You have revealed them to the childlike*, and *Unless you turn and become like children, you will not enter the kingdom of Heaven.* It's not just okay to be childlike – it's mandatory.

(Matthew 13:12): *To anyone who has, more will be given and he will grow rich: from anyone who has not, even what he has will be taken away.* There are several passages teaching that much is expected from those who have much, but this verse, when taken in context with the preceding verse 11 plus verses 13 and 14 following, refer to understanding God's words and teaching. Many in our Bible study have grown rich with Scripture and even helped others. Those who were lukewarm drifted away and probably forgot all they had learned.

The synoptic gospels of Matthew, Mark and Luke, by definition, are based on the same material. Therefore, I

Step 3 – Listen

will only address a few unique and significant passages from the other two books.

The Gospel According to Mark (Mark 3:32-33): *A crowd seated around Him told Him, your mother and brothers are outside, asking for you But He said to them in reply, "who are my mother and my brothers?* Before conversion took hold, this passage in my mind was justification for distancing myself from family. Even Jesus denied His mother and brothers was the rationale. Later, I understood that, if you permit, satan could even turn the Word of God around.

(Mark 9:23-24): *Jesus said to him, "Everything is possible to one who has faith." Then the boy's father cried out, "I do believe, help my unbelief."* On the conversion journey, we encounter almost daily proof of God's power, but also there is that lingering doubt that must be overcome. I find the last six words of great comfort and strength.

The Gospel According to Luke (Luke 1:41): *When Elizabeth heard Mary's greeting, the infant leaped in her womb.* How can any Christian tolerate abortion knowing that even in the womb, the unborn is touched by the Holy Spirit?

(Luke 4:17-21): *He unrolled the scroll and found the passage where it was written:*

The Spirit of the Lord is upon me because he has anointed me to bring glad tidings to the poor. He has sent me to proclaim liberty to captives and recovery of sight to the blind, to let the oppressed go free, Today this Scripture passage is fulfilled in your hearing.

Like Jesus, we have been anointed in Baptism and Confirmation, so we must also:

Bring the Gospel to the poor in spirit plus the necessities of life to the materially and physically poor.

Proclaim liberty to captives of satan and prisoners, including the addicted and afflicted.

Give sight to those blind to his teachings, that our calling might be fulfilled.

(Luke 11:40-42): *Martha, Martha, you are anxious and worried about many things. There is only one thing, Mary has chosen the better part and it will not be taken from her.* Too often I joked about the similarity between Martha and Valerie. Fortunately, she was quick to point out the importance of her charism of "hospitality." We must strive to understand and accept the gifts bestowed on others, not just ourselves.

(Luke 12:34): *For where your treasure is, there also your heart will be.* Review your checkbook to see where your priorities lie.

(Luke 12:47-48): *That servant who knew his masters will but did not make preparations nor act in accord with his will shall be beaten severely, and the servant who was ignorant of his masters will but acted in a way deserving of a severe beating shall be beaten only lightly. Much will be required of the person entrusted with much, and still more will be demanded of the person entrusted with more.* This may well point out the one disadvantage to praying, reading Scripture and becoming a disciple of Jesus. It is a concept that Christians discuss at length. If we learn all the truths that Jesus teaches, are we held to a higher standard? Can we no longer approach St. Peter and ask for entry into the heavenly kingdom, simply because we didn't know what God expected of us?

I believe, as C.S. Lewis discusses in "Mere Christianity," chapter 1, that there is a natural law and all humans inherently know right from wrong, even though they may not choose correctly. We Christians are called to a higher standard, to Know what God asks, or demands.

(Luke 14:12): *Jesus said, "When you hold a lunch or dinner, do not invite your friends or your brothers or your relatives or your wealthy neighbors, in case they invite you back and you have repayment.* The rewards of working at the shelter or visiting prisoners are far greater than the ephemeral pleasure of being invited to the classiest social event of the season. If we invited the poor, desperate and homeless, we might just eliminate those maladies. Valerie and I are neophytes in this arena, but with limited exposure, we both have experienced the joy of helping those that cannot help us in return or maybe even themselves.

(Luke 14:26, 27 and 33): *If anyone comes to me without hating his father and mother, wife and children, brothers and sisters, and even his own life, he cannot be my disciple. Whoever does not carry his own cross and come after me cannot be my disciple. Every one of you who does not renounce all his possessions cannot be my disciple.* This may be some of the most controversial teachings in the Gospels. Very recently, Valerie said, "You are second in my life." As disciples, Jesus <u>must</u> come first. The word *hate* may be severe in our language and possibly more understandable in the original Greek or Hebrew. When you arrive at that stage in Scripture study, it may be time to consult other translations or commentaries. Most agree that all Jesus is saying is that we dare not let anyone or anything interfere with our devotion to God.

(Luke 24:44): *"These are my words that I spoke to you while I was still with you, that everything written about me in the law of Moses and in the prophets and psalms must be fulfilled." Then He opened their minds to understand the Scriptures.* The Gospel of Luke provides wonderful justification, if we need it, for studying the Old Testament and learning about salvation history leading to the final covenant, Jesus Christ.

The Gospel According to John – John's writing is unique and often refers to Jesus as the eternal word of God. It offers much food to sustain us on the journey.

(John 2:5*)*: *His mother said to the servers: "do whatever He tells you."* Mary, the Mother of Jesus, the quintessential disciple, gives the servers, and us, the ultimate instruction, "Do whatever He tells you."

Step 3 – Listen

(John 3:30): *He must increase, I must decrease.* This was the theme of one parish's men's retreat. It touched me and most participants as a call for humility in God's presence. Men especially seem to have trouble with this.

(John 5:28-29): *The hour is coming in which all who are in the tombs will hear his voice and will come out, those who have done good deeds, to the resurrection of life.* Another Scriptural verification that it is not sufficient to say, "I accept Jesus Christ as my personal savior." We are called to do good deeds (works) predetermined by the Father. (See the section on God's Plan).

(John 6:39): *And this is the will of the one who sent me, that I should not lose anything of what he gave me, but that I should raise it on the last day.* Jesus is responsible for all of us because we were given to Him by the Father. We too are responsible for everyone given to us, even my mother-in-law.

(John 10:10): *I came so that they might have life and have it more abundantly.* He speaks not of earthly riches, but of eternal life.

(John 14:12): *Whoever believes in me will do the <u>works</u> that I do, and will do greater ones than these.* A difficult teaching to accept, but remember, with Him all things are possible.

(John 14:16 and 26): *And I will ask the Father, and He will give you another Advocate to be with you always – He will teach you everything.* A most powerful introduction to the Holy Spirit and His role in our life.

The Acts of the Apostles (Acts) – The second volume, written by Luke, was the beginning for our Little Rock Scripture Study because it deals with formation and development of our Christian/Catholic church.

(Acts 2:40): *Peter said, "save yourselves from this corrupt generation."* Sounds a bit like the 21st century and Pope John Paul II crying in the wilderness.

(Acts 2:42-47*): They devoted themselves to the teaching of the apostles and to the communal life, to the breaking of the bread and to the prayers. All who believed were together and had all things in common. Every day they devoted themselves to meeting together and to breaking bread. They ate their meals with exultation, praising God and enjoying favor, and every day the Lord added to their number those who were being saved.* This was the basis of Father Al's emphasis on Small Christian Community, a movement gaining momentum throughout the world. SCC could well be the solution to our culture of death. Unfortunately, we are not yet there, but the journey is far from over. (See also Acts 4:32-37.)

(Acts 6:4): *We shall devote ourselves to prayer and to the ministry of the Word.* We selected this for our letterhead. It may be as strong a witness as the cross I wear, or our answering machine that starts with: *May the peace of the Lord be with you.*

(Acts 10:40-41): *This man God raised on the third day and granted that he be visible, not to all the people, but to us, the witnesses chosen by God in advance, who ate and drank with him after he rose from the dead.* We who receive the Eucharist not only eat and drink with Him, but of Him, and we can do so on a daily basis if we but choose. Then we too can be witnesses, chosen by God.

After Saul's conversion the Good News was taken to the gentiles, which includes most of us. We receive it in the 21 Epistles, many of which were written by Saul after he became Paul. We will look at only a few, but as you proceed to read them, start with the introduction to each. Although not classed as inspired, it provides great insight into the letters and the writers.

The Letter to the Romans (Romans 8:16-18): *We are children of God, and if children, then heirs, heirs of God and joint heirs with Christ, if only we suffer with him so that we may also be glorified with him. I consider that the sufferings of this present time are as nothing compared with the glory to be revealed for us.* We receive an equal share with Christ – for many that means suffering; for all it means an unexplainable glory, now and forever.

(Romans 10:13-15): *Everyone who calls on the name of the Lord will be saved. But how can they call on him in whom they have not believed? And how can they believe in him of whom they have not heard? And how can they hear without someone to preach?*

And how can people preach unless they are sent? As it is written, How beautiful are the feet of those who bring the good news. One of the most beautiful calls to evangelize and spread the Gospel.

(Romans 16:1-2): *I commend to you Phoebe our sister, who is also a minister of the church at Cenchrea, that you may receive her in the Lord in a manner worthy of the holy ones, for she has been a benefactor to many and to me as well.* Finally I understood why a black Phoebe.

The First and Second Letters to the Corinthians (1 Corinthians 1:27): *God chose the foolish of the world to shame the wise, and God chose the weak of the world to shame the strong.* He chose me.

(1 Corinthians 2:9): *What eye has not seen, and ear has not heard, and what has not entered the human heart, what God has prepared for those who love him.* You ain't seen nothin' yet.

(2 Corinthians 5:19): *God was reconciling the world to himself in Christ.* Possibly the central theme of the entire New Testament.

The Letter to the Galatians (Galatians 1:9): *If anyone preaches to you a gospel other than the one you have received, let that one be accursed!* There are many dynamic Bible studies and Scripture scholars, but it is best for us to seek Catholic Scripture studies for Catholic teachings.

The Letter to the Philippians (Philippians 1:23-24): *I am caught between the two. I long to depart this*

Step 3 – Listen

life and be with Christ, for this is far better. Yet that I remain in the flesh is more necessary for your benefit. One of the last Scripture quotes received from Father Al.

The Letter to the Colossians (Colossians 2:8): *See to it that no one captivate you with an empty seductive philosophy according to human tradition, according to the elemental powers of the world and not according to Christ.* A commentary on prostitution, politics and the media (not necessarily in that order).

The Second Letter to Timothy (2 Timothy 2-16): *Avoid profane, idle talk, for such people will become more and more godless.* Justification and/or rationalization for my total lack of interest in "small talk," especially gossip.

The Letter to the Hebrews (Hebrews 10:17-18): *Their sins and evil doing I will remember no more. Where there is forgiveness of these, there is no longer offering for sin.* God forgives <u>and</u> forgets and we must do the same.

The Letter of James – About the time we were first involved with Scripture study, an associate pastor, Father George, offered a dinner table game. Each member of the group would comment on the premise that if they were confined to a desert island with only six books of the Bible, what would they be. At the time I thought, "Oh, sure." I didn't even know six books. Now I could participate and "James" would be right at the top, maybe because we seem to have a lot in common, like honesty, sometimes to a fault.

Many James passages will be used in future chapters, but for now just a few, favorite quotations, without commentary:

(James 1:22): *Be doers of the word and not hearers only.*

(James 2:5): *Did not God choose those who are poor in the world to be rich in faith and heirs of the kingdom that he promised to those who love him?*

(James 4:3): *You ask but do not receive, because you ask wrongly, to spend it on your passions.*

(James 4:6): *God resists the proud but gives grace to the humble.*

(James 4:14): *You have no idea what your life will be like tomorrow.*

(James 4:17): *For one who knows the right thing to do and does not do it, it is a sin.*

(James 5:12): *Let your "yes" mean "yes" and your "no" mean "no," that you may not incur condemnation.*

(James 5:20): *Whoever brings back a sinner from the error of his ways will save his soul from death and will cover a multitude of sins.*

Obviously, there are numerous epistles not mentioned at all. Some, along with additional portions of the Gospels will be referenced in support of future topics. One Book, the last in the Bible, Revelation, is deliberately omitted. Although we completed one study and have two additional commentaries on the subject, it appears that God has not yet opened my mind or heart to apocalyptic writing. Like I said, if you don't understand, pass it by and try again in the future. To again quote Father Al:

We need to hear God's word in the teachings of the Church

and the Bible before we "put out into deep water."

Otherwise, we would "be in over our heads."

During the very first week of promoting Bible study at St. Francis Church, an interested parishioner queried, "How long does the Bible study last?" The Holy Spirit used me to reply, without hesitation, "The rest of your life." So read the Scripture slowly. The Bible is one book that should never be finished. Someday we may be able to say that everything we need to know about life, we learned from Scripture.

Before departing this chapter, there are two additional teachings that, for me, have been truly life changing. It would be appropriate to say that these two Biblical themes have taught me to understand the meaning of life. The first I call:

Not of This World

With all that's going wrong – war, terrorism, the economy, unemployment, abortion, cloning, euthanasia, crime and even scandal in the Church – would it make you feel better if you were "not of this world?" Well, rejoice, for if you continue to believe God's word, you will shortly realize that being in this world does not sentence us to being of this world.

As mentioned in Part 1, from the time of my childhood, it was clear there must be more to life than this world offers. Later my cry became, "Is that all there is?" But now, progressing further down the steps of conversion, it is made clear that satisfaction, joy, comfort and even love does not come from this world, but from living God's kingdom here on earth. It was comforting to read what St. Paul said to the Romans in Romans 8:5-6: *For those who live according to the flesh are concerned with things of the flesh, but those who live according to the spirit with the things of the spirit. The concern of the flesh is death, but the concern of the spirit is life and peace.*

There was a time when I overused this concept. Frustrated by the misleading statements of politicians and the media, I simply reflected, thank God I'm not of this world. As it became impossible to find entertainment to enjoy with Valerie, much less the children and grandchildren, I would blame those of the world of which I was not a part. Fortunately, it soon became clear that we still must play our part in God's salvation plan, yes, for this world.

Thanks to the evangelist with multi-colored hair at major sporting events, many became aware of John 3:16, as well as verse 17: *For God so loved the world that he gave his only Son, so that everyone who believes in him might not perish but might have eternal life. For God did not send his Son into the world to condemn the world, but that the world might be saved through him.*

What did Jesus tell us about this world?:

(John 15:18-19): *If the world hates you, realize that it hated me first. If you belonged to the world, the world would love its own; but because you do not belong to the world, and I have chosen you out of the world, the world hates you.* You may not feel hated, but when we live our faith, expect to be persecuted. A friend once said, "If as a Christian you are traveling in the same direction as all others, you must be going in the wrong direction."

(John 17:14-16): *I gave them your word, and the world hated them, because they do not belong to the world any more than I belong to the world. I do not ask that you take them out of the world but that you keep them from the evil one. They do not belong to the world anymore than I belong to the world.* Jesus asks for the Father's protection even though He has already given His own.

(John 16:33): *In the world you will have trouble, but take courage, I have conquered the world.*

Shortly before the Crucifixion Jesus responded to Pilot with: *My kingdom does not belong to this world.* We are Christians and He is not of this world, so neither are we.

Later in the Epistles we find strong language about this world from St. Paul and St. John:

(1 Corinthians 15:19): *If for this life only, we have hoped in Christ, we are the most pitiable people of all.*

(1 John 3:1): *See what love the Father has bestowed on us that we may be called the children of God. Yet so we are. The reason the world does not know us is that it did not know him.*

In speaking about the antichrist, John says (1 John 4:5-6): *They belong to the world; accordingly their teaching belongs to the world, and the world listens to them. We belong to God, and anyone who knows God listens to us, while anyone who does not belong to God refuses to hear us.*

Even though we are not of this world, we must not abandon it, as Jesus did not abandon us. Even though His kingdom does not belong to this world, He still suffered and died for every person in it. We may not be ready to suffer and die for our faith, but we cannot give up. Pray always for everyone in this world to know and love He who saved. Pray for true spirituality in all people, especially the leaders, not just in politics, but for everyone we follow. Pray always – the people of this world need us more than ever. We are the Body of Christ, the hope of the world.

Made Perfect

This second life changing Biblical revelation may be the most significant, as it explains what our life should be about and how, in the end, we may be assured of salvation or at least a minimum sentence to purgatory. We are called to discover our assigned role in God's plan and the gifts we have been given, so that we may come close to the perfection our Father wishes. Let's start by considering:

When Jesus Became Perfect !!!

What!!! Isn't that blasphemy? Jesus is God, and God is perfect by definition. Didn't we learn that in the Baltimore Catechism? So why does it say in Hebrews 5:8-9: *Son though he was, he learned obedience from what he suffered; and when he was made perfect, he became the source of eternal salvation for all who obey him.* The Greek word for *perfect* is the same word meaning *mature* or *adult*. Perfect, in this sense, doesn't mean free of defects, but complete, or being all that one is supposed to be.

Jesus was born and lived His life on earth for one ultimate purpose – to suffer and die for us. Through death He became the source of eternal salvation. Possibly that explains the absence of information about the first 90 percent of His human life and very limited information about the last 10 percent, until His Passion. The part we know most about is His death on the cross, when He accomplished a role in the Father's salvation plan. Look at John 7:30: *So they tried to arrest him, but no one laid a hand on him, because his hour had not yet come.*

If we accept this, then there is an easy transition to our own lives in Christ. We too must strive for our perfection in God's plan, not to be free of flaws, but to mature in faith until we achieve what the Father has already established as our role. Look at what Jesus says to the rich young man in Matthew 19:21: *"If you wish to be perfect, sell everything and give to the poor."* The young man was not willing to accept a call for perfection, because his possessions were too important, and so he turned his back on Jesus. God probably doesn't call us to Gospel poverty, but some are called, like St. Francis and Mother Teresa, to achieve their goal without the materialism many hold so dear. We must strive to know the predetermined goal so as not to turn our backs on the Savior. We are all called to maturity, and some may even reach that perfect assignment before we are called home.

Charles Schultz, creator of Peanuts, was a very spiritual man. He tried to understand God and reflected his faith in numerous cartoon strips. We have several books that use the miniature adults to make Biblical points about life. About a week after Schultz announced retirement from cartooning, he died. I believe that Charles Schultz was put on this earth to evangelize to the masses by using creative charisms. When he decided to give it up, God welcomed home His loyal and faithful servant who had strived to fulfill his purpose.

Father Al Lauer died on October 13, 2002 at age 54. You might feel as we did, that God should not have taken this young man who was such an inspiration to

Step 3 – Listen

literally hundreds of thousands through One Bread, One Body and numerous other ministries. Truly, Father Al spent most of his life serving God's purpose. So when he achieved or came very close to his perfection, this servant was rewarded with early Heavenly retirement. He was relieved of the daily suffering of a holy man crying out in the desert of the culture of death. To quote Father Al: "In Jesus' love, death is not the end of life but the end of sin, suffering and death. In Jesus' love, death is the beginning of perfect love, peace and joy."

So if I should die shortly after completing this book, you will know what I was called to do. <u>Just kidding, Lord</u>. After all, only the good die young, or maybe only the perfect die young.

On a more serious note, let's look at what God's word says about "perfect:"

(Matthew 5:48): *So be perfect, just as your heavenly Father is perfect.*

(Romans 12:2): *Do not conform yourself to this age but be transformed by the renewal of your mind, that you may discern what is the will of God, what is good and pleasing and perfect.*

(1 Corinthians 13:10. Read also verse 11): *But when the perfect comes, the partial will pass away.*

(2 Corinthians 12:9): *My grace is sufficient for you, for power is made perfect in weakness.*

(Philippians 3:14-15): *I continue my pursuit towards the goal, the prize of God's upward calling, in Christ*

Jesus. Let us, then, who are "perfectly mature" adopt this attitude.

(Colossians 3:14): *Put on love, that is the bond of perfection.*

(James 1:4): *And let perseverance be perfect, so that you may be perfect and complete, lacking in nothing.*

(1 John 4:12): *God remains in us, and his love is brought to perfection in us.*

Most or maybe all of us want to look back on our lives with satisfaction. The ultimate reward comes from doing the good works that God has predestined, and just maybe we, too, will be made perfect. Is it impossible for mere humans to reach perfection? Yes, but trusting in Him and being completely dependent on Him, *we can do greater things than even Jesus has done* (John 14:12). Striving for perfection is the way to purification. Must we achieve perfection for salvation? Probably not, but we should come before God trying. We seek to understand God's plan for us and try our best to discern and use the gifts given to us by the Holy Spirit.

Step 4 – God's Plan

So what is this, "God's Plan"? Is it specific for each individual? Is it dependent on others in your life? Or, as discussed by many theologians, are we all part of the Father's salvation plan, starting with Adam and culminating with the final coming and judgment? I believe the answer to all these questions is "yes." That sounds pretty heavy. How can little old, insignificant me have a part in this grand endeavor. To again quote Father Al, "We Christians belong to a team that is the Body of Christ, and God has set each member in the place He wanted you to be. Therefore, it is critical to know and fulfill our designated role, no more, no less, as best we can."

John Paul II, writing in preparation for the third millennium, put it very succinctly: "Be docile to the Holy Spirit." Webster defines docile as "willing to obey." It may be more like "trying to know and obey."

Do you believe that the Lord has chosen you to be great? You should, because you are His child; we are all His children. You are so important that you cannot become more important through your own efforts. If you really want to make God laugh, just tell Him what you are planning for your life. On the contrary, if God revealed His plan for you, you would swear He had your file mixed up with the Pope or maybe one of the saints. That's how I felt when first trying to understand where I fit in that marvelous plan.

As mentioned earlier, why would He pick someone to start a parish Bible study who knew little or nothing about Scripture. Easy! This is the "good works" planned for me for the benefit of others. It helps if we quit looking at significant milestones as mere coincidence and begin recognizing them as "God-incidence."

Another revelation in God's plan occurred when I began looking back to see that He had been directing my life toward His goal, if I didn't resist. Let me share just a few of the events, some from Part 1, that were not obvious at first occurrence:

When first divorced, our youngest child was just 5. I made an unspoken commitment that no one would come between my three children and me until the children were all adults. Shortly before Mark turned 18, God sent Valerie into my life.

About six months before we met, God removed my 32-year addiction to cigarettes. Valerie's husband, a smoker, had died of lung cancer. She would not have been willing to go through that again. Although she willingly married me knowing of my alcoholism,

Step 4 – God's Plan

through her love and prayers He took way the second addiction.

In response to a novena, we were led to Vista and a property saved for us for over 13 years.

Our parish leaders chose a Bible illiterate to start their Scripture study.

My journals of God-incidence now encompass three volumes. Look back on your life for a supreme pattern, and then move forward in His plan.

Must we cooperate? Let's look at two somewhat hypothetical possibilities. The first deals with two people well aware of His plan who make a conscious but contrary decision. The second reveals a couple, not unlike most cradle Catholics, not really knowing or understanding the concept of God's plan:

Let's say that God's plan for Valerie and me is to lead a comfortable and holy life here in Vista. We are to concentrate on loving each other and everyone that God puts into our lives, nurturing our family, witnessing to them and our neighbors, being responsible for certain ministries like Bible study (LRSS) and the cancer support group (SPAN), plus being active in Jesus' body on earth, the church. His plan is easy and joyful, in His presence. You might say we have an abundant life.

Suppose we depart from that plan, for example, by taking an extended vacation that interferes with our designated role in family, community and the church. Even though we make other arrangements for our major ministries, we are not there to lead as chosen.

Let's say that our trip takes us as far as New York City and on 9/11/01 we are enjoying a gourmet breakfast at the top of the World Trade Center. Did God cause our death, or was it allowed because we chose our own way? Maybe most of the people destroyed in that event were fugitives from God's plan. We now became part of something that many believe was a wake-up call for America. Will it have more impact on the citizens of Vista because of who we were? Do we go to hell without the opportunity to repent or, as many believe, did we have a last chance for reconciliation while the gasoline flames surrounded us? Maybe all of those on the road to perdition are refuges from God's plan who refused the opportunity for repentance???????

Let's look at a slightly less frightening example. What if a young couple of cradle Catholics falls in love and get married? For the next 15 years they co-exist in lukewarm faith. God blesses them with three beautiful children. Finally frustrated by their lack of commitment, God, with the couples' cooperation, allows satan into their lives, he through alcohol and she due to an interest in the occult. The result is a bitter and painful divorce and subsequent annulment. Did God abandon His plan for the two? I think not. It became apparent they were not going to achieve perfection together, so the plan was allowed to change.

Later she repented and came back to the church in a very active way. In addition, when her family of adult children and grandchildren needed her most, she was there in a very positive way. The man continued his alcoholic ways for about 15 years, until God led him to a widow who, through prayer and support, would help overcome the addiction. Now as husband and wife they strive to live God's plan on a daily basis. So why didn't the Father put them together shortly after his failed relationship? Two possibilities – he may have needed the 15 years of purgatory, and the obvious, she was busy helping to convert her first husband to Catholicism. No matter how good you are, God only allows you to work with one spouse at a time.

Let us now look at what God says about His plan in His own words:

(Amos 3:7): *The Lord God does nothing without revealing his plan to his servants, the prophets.* Father Al always exhorted us to seek all the gifts, but above all the gift of prophecy.

(Genesis 50:20): *Joseph said to his brothers, "Even though you meant harm to me, God meant it for good, to achieve his present end, the survival of many people."* Read the whole story of Joseph and his family, and see God's plan unfold. This tale is the basis for "Joseph and His Amazing Technicolor Dream Coat."

(Ephesians 2:10): *For we are his handiwork, created in Christ Jesus for the good works that God has prepared in advance, that we should live in them.*

(2 Corinthians 9:7): *Each must do as already determined.*

(Ephesians 1:9-10): *He has made known to us the mystery of his will in accord with his favor that he has set forth in him as a plan for the fullness of times.*

Paul in his farewell speech at Miletus acknowledges the significance of God's plan (Acts 20:24): *Yet I consider life of no importance to me, if only I may finish my course and the ministry that I received from the Lord Jesus,*

So let us pray daily: Father, may I live the life of good works for which you have created me. May every detail of your plan for my life be fulfilled.

Step 5 – Gifts

Probably the easiest way to begin recognizing God's plan for your life is to identify the gifts He has given. After all, we cannot expect to do the pre-planned good works without being adequately equipped. God loves us and wants us to succeed, so it follows that we will be graced with everything required. Success comes when we recognize and begin to exercise these very unique graces.

Most understand and give the Lord credit for certain talents. We often say that someone is a gifted athlete, musician or even cook. Yes, the home-based talents can be part of a supernatural gift of, say, "Hospitality," specifically identified in Scripture.

But let's not get ahead of ourselves. Let us first look at the types of gifts He bestows. As taught in the Catechism of the Catholic Church, these gifts are:

The Gifts of the Holy Spirit, which are supernatural graces freely given to the soul with sanctifying grace. These seven gifts are wisdom, understanding, counsel, fortitude, knowledge, piety, and fear of the Lord. (Catechism of the Catholic Church (CCC) (1831.)

Charisms are the extraordinary gifts or graces of the Holy Spirit given to individuals <u>for the sake of others</u> (CCC 799-801).

The key distinction is that the latter is given for the sake of others, more often called community, for the glory of God. For example, the charism allowing someone to be a talented musician is probably best used in the church choir as opposed to sitting alone, playing the guitar for self-gratification. Those of us believing the Holy Spirit wishes to awaken Catholics to His gifts are often called Charismatics. This term is scary to many in our faith who look only at the hand waving, loud singing individuals who often seem to mutter in some indistinguishable language (tongues). Truth be known, that when you begin to seek the specific God-given gifts that make each unique, you, too become a charismatic. We cannot fulfill His plan without recognizing our charisms.

Another distinction made by various sources is in the number of such graces. Most traditionalists will recognize the seven gifts of the Holy Spirit revealed to Isaiah and used in the Confirmation ceremony. The following definitions are taken from a book of "Devotions to the Holy Spirit:"

> <u>Wisdom</u> – of God which shows mere human wisdom to be folly.

Understanding – is spiritual insight that guards us against spiritual shallowness.

Counsel – is a maturity of judgment guarding against imprudent action or judgment.

Knowledge – of the things of God and His ways with humans.

Fortitude – courage that bears all things, hopes all things and sustains all things.

Piety – that deep sense of reverence for God in all His wonder.

Fear of the Lord – The fear one has who is deeply in love and greatly loved, and fears to do anything that will diminish that love in any way.

Father Al Lauer acknowledges these seven and discusses an additional 24, including: Prophecy, Faith, Ministry, Teaching, Exhortation, Giving, Leadership, Mercy, Healing, Miracles, Discernment of Spirits, Tongues, Interpretation of Tongues, Apostles/Disciples, Helpers, Administrators, Martyrdom, Evangelists, Pastors, Deliverance, Celibacy, Gospel Poverty, Intercession, and Hospitality. Biblical references and descriptions for all 31 may be found in Father's booklet, " Seek The Gifts Of The Spirit."

About two years ago, Valerie and I, along with some 30 other St. Francis parishioners, participated in a weekend, "Called and Gifted Workshop." Through a series of lectures and simple questions, we came to recognize our most dominant, God given talents.

In addition to identifying our gifts, we also learned to verify their authenticity as being from the Holy Spirit. It came as no surprise that the results showed my most dominant charism to be "writing." For much of my career I wrote proposals to the government and aerospace prime contractors, resulting in numerous contracts for my employer. You might say that many fellow employees benefited from my gift, but I'm not sure that's what God had in mind.

The workshop, however, prompted me to begin work on this book, a gift from the Holy Spirit, for the benefit of community and the glory of God. At times the words and thoughts came so fast that is was like taking dictation from a higher power. When complete, it will be up to the Spirit to see that it gets in the hands of his chosen audience.

Before moving on, let me share a few more personal or plagiarized observations on Gifts and Charisms:

Don't try to do what God has not gifted you for. Had I listened, it would have saved my parents hundreds of dollars and days of excruciating ear pain before admitting that talent with the saxophone was not my gift. If we yearn for a different role than God has assigned, we miss the joy of serving as He has chosen.

One of the most important, yet most difficult of gifts, especially for Catholics, is "Evangelization."

Step 5 – Gifts

We have enough difficulty letting Jesus become a significant element in our lives, much less encouraging others to do the same, and yet it's really quite simple. Evangelization is nothing more than sharing your own story. Simply pick an event in your life when you recognized the presence of God, something that occurred without the appearance of divine intervention. It doesn't need to be miraculous. In fact, it's probably better that it's not so people can readily accept the story. Then look for every opportunity to fit it into conversation with others. That's evangelization.

The following is my personal favorite, shared numerous times. The story not only gets a laugh but a great deal of amazed recognition. As you will also see, the Pastor exhibits the gift of prophecy:

Each year, starting just before Christmas, the San Diego Wild Animal Park holds an evening celebration of lights, which includes arts and crafts plus numerous other activities for the children. This year, like previous ones, we were due to meet our family from Ramona, including three active young grandsons. We had just been to one family gathering and were scheduled for another in a couple of days, so I was less than enthusiastic about the Wild Animal Park outing. The morning of the event, I asked Valerie to call and say we would not be going. She accepted my plea.

I then departed for morning Mass at St. Margaret's church, for some reason, alone. During the short drive, I was experiencing good old Catholic guilt about not fulfilling my grandfatherly duties. The Pastor, Father Bill Gold, finished reading the Gospel and moved closer to the congregation for a short homily. I nearly fainted when he began with, "You should go to the Wild Animal Park in the evening." The only thing missing was, "Joe."

I don't recall the real point of his homily, but for me the message was clear. Valerie was also shocked by the homily story but glad we would be participating in another family gathering. Neither of us was prepared for the call from Deb explaining that all three sons were tired, and they were going to skip the festivities. We had a saying in sales, "You get as many points offering to take someone to lunch as you do actually taking them." It's not clear what point God was making, but there was no doubt about divine intervention.

Probably the most important gift for our personal growth is discernment, the ability to allow God to guide your decision making. It is also one of the most difficult charisms to cultivate, often because our own ego gets in the way. Yet without it we may end up following the wrong lead. The gift is also called "Discernment of Spirits," the ability to distinguish between the Holy Spirit, an evil spirit and our own human spirit. Obviously, it's crucial to know which is doing the guiding.

For example, Valerie has considered selling this house and buying a larger property where we can provide temporary housing for unwed expectant

Step 5 – Gifts

mothers to help them avoid the mortal sin of killing through abortion. Certainly this is a holy and noble idea, and it's unlikely that the devil would lead us in that direction. But remember, our home and location, we believe, was provided by God in response to a novena of prayers. It's most likely where He wants us to be. So maybe the thought of relocating to help the needy is a wonderful but human inclination from a good and compassionate woman, but not where God is calling her.

As mentioned, it's not the easiest of gifts and requires continuous prayer. "Father, may I live the life of good works for which you have created me."

One last tip. Since all charisms are given for the benefit of community, it makes sense to pray for guidance with others. In the example above, Valerie and I must pray together for discernment on a matter that greatly impacts both of us.

The final charism, which I'll discuss at some length, is the one that Father Al considered to be above all others. He encouraged everyone, regardless of what gifts God had given you, to "seek prophecy." It is, however, one of the most misunderstood graces. Prophecy is not future telling, as so many think it is. Remember, it is a gift from God – fortune telling is not. It has nothing to do with psychics, tarot cards, crystal balls, or other tools of the occult, all of which we know *is an abomination to the Lord*. It is, rather, a communication from God, given to one individual to be relayed to others, for their benefit.

The prophets of the Old Testament were usually tasked with giving God's instructions on life to the nations of Israel, especially if they were doing something wrong. In many cases the Jews did not want to be reprimanded, even by a spokesperson for Yahweh, and they would rebel, sometime even killing the prophets. Jesus, we know, was considered by some Jews to be only the ultimate prophet. But unlike the prophets, Jesus spoke for Himself, as God, often beginning with, *"amen amen, I say to you."*

Being a public relations representative for God is so significant that many may fool themselves into believing they have the gift. Most "praise and worship" services end with a small stream of people coming to the ambo, professing words that God supposedly gave them for the congregation. I must confess to a lack of confidence in the authenticity of the source. Most prophet wannabes begin their moment in the spotlight with "my children or my people." Most prophets in Scripture give proper credit to the source, saying something like "the Lord God says" or "the Lord of Hosts says." Hopefully, it's my unbelief rather than the fault of these modern-day prophets. Their message is not false but may lack complete discernment. Remember, if you have not received, do not try to use the gift.

I have never laid claim to the gift of prophecy nor, in spite of my great love for Father Al, did I actively pursue that special blessing. Possibly, my reluctance is based on a fear that I might utter human, not Godly, communication. However, since I recognize this writing as a gift from the Holy Spirit, it might well be one lengthy prophetic message destined for one or more recipients chosen by God.

Should you be blessed with representing God to others, do not be surprised if those closest to you do not accept your role. Following is an entire daily meditation written by Father Al for OBOB on July 6, 2003:

GOD SPEAKS THROUGH PEOPLE WE DON'T LISTEN TO

"No prophet is without honor except in his native place, among his own kindred, and in his own house." –Mark 6:4

The church was born at Pentecost as the prophet Joel's prophecy about prophecy was fulfilled. Immediately after our Baptisms, we were anointed with the chrism oil as priests, prophets, and kings. This indicates the centrality and importance of prophecy in God's plan of salvation. The Church is even founded on the apostles and the prophets (Ephesians 2:20). Thus, the Lord commands us to seek zealously the spiritual gifts, "above all, the gift of prophecy (1 Corinthians 14:1).

Prophecy means to give a message from God. However, to give we must receive, that is, listen and obey. Yet prophets are traditionally not received and listened to, especially in their native places (Mark

6:4), which is where the Lord usually sends them. Thus, the initial key to our prophetic ministry is to listen to the Lord speaking through those closest to us. For example, if a man doesn't hear God speaking through his wife, how can he be a prophet or even a Christian in touch with the Lord? If we don't hear God speaking through our parents, how can we hear God at all?

Listen to God speaking through those closest to you, who are often the most difficult for you to listen to. Then prophesy.

Prayer: Father, may I listen to You speaking through the person I can't stand to hear.
Promise: "Therefore, I am content with weakness, with mistreatment, with distress, with persecutions, and difficulties for the sake of Christ; for when I am powerless, it is then that I am strong." – 2 Corinthians 12:10
Praise: Praise Jesus, our Life, Resurrection, and only Hope!

If you knew me from my early years and read this book, you might be tempted to say, "Isn't that Joseph, the son of John, the assembly worker, and Julia, the housewife? Where does he get off professing such words?" I don't. It's a gift.

In Part I, I mentioned several instances where someone had a prophetic word for me. It was prophecy that led us to Vista and St. Francis of Assisi Church, prophecy that gave me my first copy of OBOB

Step 5 – Gifts

and subsequently led us to discipleship retreats at Presentation Ministries. Through prayer and docility to the Holy Spirit, we have accepted many revelations that came in various forms – from Scripture, obviously, but also from other holy writings, lectures and most especially homilies.

Even after his death, we still consider Father Al our personal prophet. His meditations for OBOB were written two to three years in advance, and so the enlightenment will continue for some time. After that I just may start over, having saved every copy. Or God may choose to send us another Paraclete. Hardly a week goes by where Valerie and I are not blessed with guidance from above.

And lest we forget, there is the direct representative of the Holy Spirit still visiting in our own back yard – Phoebe!

We had a very recent example of God's loving guidance. It was a day when we were having a significant difference of opinion (argument to some). During Mass, Father Pat's homily beautifully addressed the unresolved issues. Naturally, the Scripture supported his position, as it should.

Father Al's meditation from OBOB prophetically dealt with the same subject. While we were sitting on the patio, sharing a Jack-in-the-Box croissant sandwich, Phoebe stopped by for an affirming visit. She was chirping more than usual, as if to say, "Well, I hope you got all of that." Just so there is no misunderstanding,

Phoebe did not partake in even the smallest crumb. We have never attempted to bribe her and figure the Holy Spirit, even as a small bird, is capable of taking care of herself.

So pray always to become a prophet, but also to hear, understand and accept the words meant just for you. Wherever you are, in the near occasion of God's grace, in church, home, at work or school, listen intently to what is said or pay particular attention to what you read. God may well be providing divine guidance. Then pray for the faith, hope, love and trust to follow wherever He leads.

Let's now share a few of the passages that lead us to understand God's plan and gifts in our lives:

(Deuteronomy 18:21-22): *How can we recognize an oracle which the Lord has spoken? If his oracle is not fulfilled or verified, it is an oracle which the Lord did not speak.*

(Mark 6:4-5): *Jesus said to them, "A prophet is not without honor except in his native place and among his own kin and in his own house." So He was not able to perform any mighty deeds there.*

(Acts 2:4): *And they were filled with the Holy Spirit and began to speak in different tongues.*

(Acts 19:6): *And when Paul laid hands on them, the Holy Spirit came upon them and they spoke in tongues and prophesied.*

(1 Corinthians 12:7-11): *To one is given through the spirit the expression of wisdom, to another the*

expression of knowledge, to another faith, to another gifts of healing, to another mighty deeds, to another prophecy, to another discernment of spirits, to another tongues, to another interpretation of tongues. But one and the same Spirit produces all of these, distributing them individually to each person <u>as he wishes.</u>

(1 Corinthians 12:31): *Strive eagerly for the greatest spiritual gifts.*

(Hebrews 2:4): *God added His testimony by signs, wonders, various acts of power, and distribution of the gifts of the Holy Spirit according to His will.*

(2 Peter 1:20-21): *Know this first of all, that there is no prophecy of Scripture that is a matter of personal interpretation, for no prophecy ever came through human will.*

Seek the Gifts of the Spirit.

There is another category of gifts or blessings that may not qualify as charisms. Like those that are spiritual, the others, also from God, affect more our physical, mental and emotional state and development, and must be used appropriately. I call these gifts "abundances and limitations." Looking carefully we might discover a relationship between these and our charisms.

An extreme example might be a Down's syndrome child. There are the obvious physical and developmental limitations, but have you ever noticed the abundance of love that radiates from their smiles and hugs?

Another more common example can be seen in our senior community, with many like my neighbor, who although more than 10 years older than I am, has an abundance of physical energy which he constantly uses to improve the appearance and comfort of his home. He often challenges others to keep up. However, if I were blessed with his energy, it might have limited the abundance of patience God gave me over the past three years while working on this manuscript.

For many, like Valerie and me, we must recognize that less than abundant energy is a limitation that is also a blessing. Our Lord is saying, "Slow down, listen, look and learn what I ask of you." As mentioned, Valerie's chemotherapy caused her to slow down, maybe so I could keep up. We need to slow down to allow the Holy Spirit to catch up. There is even a bumper sticker that reads: "Never Drive Faster Than Your Guardian Angel Can Fly." God has tasks for us at different times in our lives, and so He changes our abundances and our limitations.

I wonder, sometime, if we are living longer because we need more time to recognize and overcome the culture of death. There is an old saying, "Youth is a wonderful thing, but it's a shame it is wasted on the young." Maybe if we began working on our conversion earlier, we would not have to panic and cram for the finals. You might say, "Blessed are the old in spirit, for they may sooner reach perfection."

Step 5 – Gifts

Scripture tells us, *"When I was a child, I used to talk as a child, think as a child, reason as a child; when I became a man, I put aside childish things."* (1 Corinthians 13:11). We are called to be childlike, not childish. Is it time to end the childlike use of "abundances and limitations" and begin to use a childlike nature to follow Jesus? Just as with charisms, we must strive to use these other, more recognizable gifts for the promotion of God's Kingdom on earth and for the benefit of our brothers and sisters.

Step 6 – Lifestyle

In this section we look at participating in the church as a major part of our lifestyle. We will consider my role and your role in both the physical and spiritual church, the Body of Christ here on earth. Many good and would be Catholics are struggling because of the current scandals in the priesthood, and rightfully so. Before discussing getting more involved with your parish, let me share some of my thoughts and others that have been shared with me.

I was angry, I was hurt, I was disappointed, but most of all I felt abandoned, not by our Father in Heaven but by many of the fathers here on earth. Just when my public ministry was beginning, the leaders of our faith had made it extremely difficult to evangelize about Catholicism. Thank God that my faith had matured, so there was no question as to where shall I go but what can I do. It was clear there were many good and holy members of the clergy that also felt abandoned and needed support. How could I explain to others,

Step 6 – Lifestyle

especially weak or non-Catholics, when I did not fully understand myself.

It was easier to understand and forgive the sick, human priest guilty of the molestations than to justify the church hierarchy who continue to this day to hide the flaws and continue to place many in the near occasion of sin. I became angrier when one of my heroes at SCRC gave a long talk placing most of the blame on the media. True, I have little respect for the media, but my church was giving them, through our sinfulness, the material for their reports. I lashed out in letters to our local Bishop and another Archbishop we had met, who at one time had been president of the National Conference of Catholic Bishops. The responses were predictable and less than satisfying. Even now, the Vatican has not adequately addressed the issue, at least not to those of us who are considered their flock.

The healing for me came because I could not abandon Jesus Christ, the true head of my Church. He led me in Scripture and in homilies from local priests to a fuller understanding – not an excuse, but an understanding. Ever so often in the history of Catholicism, a cross is given for us loyal followers to carry. This scandal is our current cross, and we must bear this burden, since we are now His body.

Reflect for a moment on the treatise of becoming perfect. It took Jesus His entire life to reach perfection. If you're like me, we are a long, long way from our ultimate goal. But now we know that our priests are not perfect, our bishops are not perfect, our cardinals are not perfect, and, I venture a guess, our Pope has not yet reached perfection. We are all sinners. Let us remember that Jesus did not come to minister to perfect people, He came to teach sinners; He came to serve and to save sinners. He even chose sinners to be part of His inner circle. So is it any wonder He continues to choose sinners? Be grateful; otherwise, He cannot choose us. The scandals prove that the chosen people of Israel did not have a monopoly on disobedience. Remember also that the closer we get to God, the more we will be attacked by evil forces. It follows then that our deacons, priests, bishops, cardinals and especially the Pope must be under constant bombardment from the legion of darkness. That is why we must continue support, prayer and unconditional love.

Jesus and His apostles warned us to expect such scandals and evil attacks in the church. For starters, open your Bible to what Paul said to early church leaders in the letters to Timothy and Titus. In addition, let's consider a few other pertinent passages from Scripture:

(Hebrews 7:28): *For the law appoints men subject to weakness to be high priests, but the word of the oath, which was taken after the law, appoints a son, who has been made perfect forever.*

(1 John 2:18-19): *It is the last hour; and just as you heard that the antichrist was coming, so now many antichrists have appeared. They went out from us, but*

they were not really of our number, if they had been, they would have remained with us.

(2 Corinthians 11:14-15): *For even satan masquerades as an angel of light. So it is not strange that his ministers also masquerade as ministers of righteousness.*

Paul, in his letter to the Romans (Romans 1:18-32), titled "Punishment of Idolaters," becomes very graphic about sins of lust and homosexuality that seemed to contribute to these scandals. But be not afraid, for Jesus promised our church would survive, when He said to Peter, *"You are Peter, and upon this rock I will build this church, and the gates of the netherworld shall not prevail against it"* (Matthew 16:18). Remember, ours is a faith of love, forgiveness and reconciliation. Jesus died for all sinners.

With that said, we can move onto examining our lifestyle, including involvement with our Catholic church. Now that we are aware of the tools given by God, how can they be used in a new life apart from this secular world and culture of death? The answer in one short phrase: "Be docile to the Holy Spirit." At the same time, when we ask for guidance and strength in spirituality, holiness, trust, etc., we cannot just sit back and expect the Father to simply grant our petitions. We must also participate. Begin living as if God has already acted in your life, for He has. If you pray to believe, believe. If you pray to be happy, be happy. If you pray to do good works, start doing good works.

Granted not all changes are that simple. For many like myself up to 12 years ago, a sinful lifestyle can become addictive and require fervent prayer by us and those who support us. We may also need to seek professional help, which may be available through the church. But for most there are numerous lifestyle changes not requiring long periods of discernment meditation. They are what our younger generations call "no-brainers." For example, Jesus tells us to "pray" "always." He tells us to love, unconditionally, also to avoid sin, help the poor and visit the sick. If we start with the easy tasks that we know are pleasing to our Lord, He will begin helping with the more difficult. It's easier to give the first 98 percent of our lives than to give the last two percent. I guess the devil makes a goal line stand.

It appears that God granted me freedom from one very large, sinful addiction, alcohol, so that my mind became clear to see what else He offered. Even with that weight lifted, it took several years for the conversion process to start when I opened my heart and called personally to the Spirit. But God is prompting us to avoid those years of struggle by surrendering and living in the Kingdom now.

Shortly after our marriage, Valerie introduced me to a word that has had a significant impact on our day-to-day life. The term is "crabgrass." Whenever we find ourselves spending an inordinate amount of energy on something not worthy of our God given-time, talent

Step 6 – Lifestyle

or treasure, she would immediately say, "crabgrass." This was the prompting to quit cultivating the weeds. Examples might be idle conversation that can easily lead to gossip (see 2 Timothy 2:16), or watching too much TV and movies, also reading meaningless fiction and often even non-fiction. There is crabgrass in all our lives. The secret is to identify it, rip it out and refuse to allow it to spread. Recently, I was told the term is frequently used in the Marriage Encounter program.

For years, especially while drinking, I spent a lot of precious, God given-time fertilizing crabgrass. Much of my so-called free time was engaged in watching sports, to which I had no connection or real interest in the outcome. Then there was fiction reading, which after many hours left me with a feeling of emptiness, wondering why I had even bothered.

There is a lot of crabgrass in the world that satan keeps neatly manicured so that it appears as expensive sod, worthy of our admiration, but it's still crabgrass. Begin today eliminating, little by little, the weeds that choke out the real meaning of life in the Kingdom. Be preoccupied with Jesus, even though it's not always easy. At the beginning of prayer or Scripture reading, the devil begins to sow the seeds of distraction. Persevere and ask the Lord to strengthen you to know the beautiful blossoms of His Spirit alone.

Many of us cradle Catholics are what we are because of parents, spouse, other relatives or even the church community. That's the good news. Unfortunately, we may be at our current faith level due to the influence of the "culture of death" in which we live. For example, even though we may be adamantly against abortion, euthanasia and homosexuality, we don't relate that to being entertained by movies or TV glorifying those same sins. We cast ballots for politicians seriously lacking in many proper moral and religious values, justifying the action with, "that's what everyone else is doing." I admit to having selected candidates because they were the "lesser of two evils" and then being disappointed when they turned out to be just that, "the lesser of two evils." What a change could occur if all Catholics based their actions on God-given principles. Miracles do happen!

Father Al frequently used the word "radical" in regard to the lifestyle we are called to lead. Others would call his teaching fanatical. One dictionary defines "fanatic" as "excessive enthusiasm." Wanting what God asks of us should not be considered excessive, but more like "just right." Radical is defined as going to the foundation of something fundamental. God's instructions must be considered the fundamental basis for life. God is not just giving us suggestions, but responsibilities for which we are held accountable. We may not be ready to identify our style as radical or fanatical, but we are to be disciples, and, simply stated, discipleship is "following the teachings and example of Jesus Christ" to which we are all called.

Step 6 – Lifestyle

Let's take a look at my version of the lifestyle of many typical cradle Catholics. This is a simple task since it represents the first 90 percent of my own life. But my example should not be used as an excuse to delay starting the conversion journey. God has blessed me, so far, with 68 years to get it right. Not everyone will have that luxury.

We arise in the morning, shower and dress. Some will put on a cross, crucifix or holy medal, under our clothes, so no one can see it. Our breakfast may or may not be preceded by a prayer of thanksgiving. Chances are the whole family is not at the table. Parents and children will not hug, express their love and wish each other God's blessing before rushing off to their separate worlds. In the car we listen to the news or the popular talk show, not even aware that there are Christian stations teaching God's word of encouragement, 24 hours a day. We manage to make it through eight or more hours of work without ever mentioning our faith or thanking God for our many blessings. At lunch we are too embarrassed for grace in public.

On the way home we listen again to the news to find what satan has been able to accomplish since morning. Maybe the evening meal includes the whole family, the TV is off and we start with a prayer. Unfortunately, many families do not take time for this ritual because the kids must get off to soccer practice, little league, or some other activity that "everyone else is doing." But that's okay, because then the adults have time to read the same news or see it on TV, complete with graphic pictures. Later the family gathers for an hour or two of sitcoms not suitable for the parents, much less the children. Or they may separate to seek, in private, their individual vices and addictions on a smaller screen.

On Sunday many families sit in on Mass, although if you look around, you might believe there are many more single women, with and without children, than whole families. The Mass we select is often dictated by plans for shopping trips or TV sporting events. Does this all seem a bit negative? For your family I pray that it is.

For comparison, let's look at what life might be like for the family of a disciple in training. Not an evangelizing charismatic, but a simple everyday kind of Catholic just beginning to seek the real meaning of life. This also is familiar to me because it more closely represents my thoughts, beliefs and actions for the most recent part of my life, as my love for God continues to grow. Make no mistake – our faith and love must grow or else it dies; there is no status quo in conversion.

When first our eyes open in the morning, we praise and thank our maker for another day. The first 10 minutes or more of each day are devoted to prayer and Scripture, to see what prophetic word the Lord is offering for guidance. The whole family shares a prayer and breakfast meal plus a sign of love before we go our separate ways. Our time in transit allows for more conversation with our Leader. A long commute is ideal

Step 6 – Lifestyle

for the rosary. Even a short trip will accommodate a decade or two. Maybe you have the need for news or a traffic report. In my section of the country, that need is also satisfied by the Christian stations. You might be surprised how much more positive the events sound when the presenter is working for the Lord.

We think about God, frequently, during the day. Ask for help to overcome the turmoil, and thank Him for those little and big successes. During the lunch break, thank God again, publicly, for the nourishment. Bring along your Bible to read during those free moments or simply as a sign of witness. You might be surprised by an associate who shares your belief but was reluctant to admit it. Many are not ready for verbal evangelization, but that Bible and the medal worn on the outside of your clothing will speak volumes. Take the risk of offending a friend by suggesting they not take our Lord's name in vain. Our neighbor still thanks us for making him aware of a sinful but unintentional habit.

On the way home, look forward to an evening with family. Share how God acted in your life this day. In addition to grace before meals, we might ask each member to reveal what they are particularly thankful for. This works well with large gatherings for special occasions. In every family there are difficult issues that must be addressed. Once when Valerie and I were having a particularly difficult time, we sought the help of a local priest who doubled as a family counselor. His advice: set time aside, at day's end, for discussion, but always begin with a prayer requesting the intercession of the Holy Spirit. It works – not just in times of strife, but also for discerning family options.

Regarding the family's evening entertainment, my opinion about TV, movies and the Internet has been formed by two of my favorite holy men, Father Al, of course, and Father Benedict Groeshel, often seen on EWTN. They all may have some redeeming value, but the garbage we must sift through makes them hardly worthwhile. To, again, quote Father Al, "Many don't see that they are being programmed by a culture of death. They stare at TV (movies or the Internet) and become brainwashed, anesthetized, and spiritually paralyzed."

EWTN, as mentioned, stands for "The Eternal Word Television Network," available through Dish Network and many cable providers. The all-Catholic station, founded by Mother Angelica, offers news, children and young adult shows, plus a large variety of presenters to inform and challenge Catholics at all levels. They even provide daily Mass, the rosary and ongoing Bible studies. Just remember that the TV Mass does not satisfy the Sabbath requirement, and the study programs are not a substitute for the faith-filled interaction of parish gatherings. Another benefit of EWTN – no commercials, except for a few promoting the glory of being Christian.

Let's end the day as we started: praising, loving and thanking God, in your own words, for all He has put in your life, especially the people. Admittedly, with my personal weakness, I ask God for the strength to love everyone He has given me, unconditionally, plus to know and love God more and more each day. Remember, grow or die. Whatever happened to that wonderful old saying, " The family that prays together, stays together"? And don't neglect the hugs and kisses.

Does this all seem a bit overwhelming? Is it so foreign from how most of us live that we can't imagine the radical change? What makes it challenging is the departure from the way most people lead their lives. It's not like life on the sitcoms, or what the commercials present, but remember, those things are of this world and we, converted Catholics, are not. We are created for greater, if we let God lead our lives.

The Body of Christ

So we have looked at the very limited activity of the Sunday-go-to-church, cradle Catholic. It's not enough to ignore the culture of death – we must join a community of life.

For me that help, strength, encouragement comes through our Savior, in the company of a holy community, our parish. As mentioned, Valerie facilitates a Christian cancer support group, and that is precisely the role of the parish church. It is a Catholic cancer support group, but in this case the cancer is the society in which we live. But, not only does the church provide support, it can also guarantee a 100 percent healing.

Sound radical? Well, let's see how radically a lifestyle can change through participation in a faith-based fellowship. Admittedly, the Catholic faith is not easy. It's not meant to be. Remember, it's the church started by Jesus, who suffered abuse and excruciating pain, eventually dying a most humiliating death on the cross, so that we may be saved. The apostles were all martyred for their beliefs. Our Savior even called us to share in carrying the cross, so why should we expect any less from His church, the Body of Christ, here on earth? That is why so many choose something less. That is why there are so many alternative Christian religious rites. That is why there is an abundance of "feel good" churches that do not teach the entire truth. Only the Catholic church offers the presence of Christ in the Eucharist, His Body, Blood, Soul and Divinity, <u>on a daily basis.</u> But remember, because God gave us so much, He expects more from us. The Catholic faith is an adult, mature faith. Maybe that's why Jesus didn't begin His ministry to us until He was in His 30s. Someone said," Immature religion is the best place to avoid God.

The truth is, the Catholic faith *is easy and the burden light.* For with the love of the Father, the guidance of the Holy Spirit, the grace of receiving Jesus into our body, mind, heart and soul, coupled with support of the Catholic community, there is strength to endure

Step 6 – Lifestyle

any hardship. If you're going to be a Christian, why not belong to the church Christ started. So pray, as I do, "Father, thank you for opening my heart to finally accept your truth and thereby receiving a life worth living, forever, Alleluia, Amen."

The next and most important step in maturing our lifestyle is to get involved with your Catholic church. Play an active role in the parish family. The rewards will be greater than you can possibly imagine. How do we start? Our parish, St. Francis of Assisi, offers some 46 different stewardship opportunities, from parish office help to youth groups, assisting at Mass as a reader, or distributing the Sacred Body and Blood, plus service groups like jail, home and hospital visits, and of course, Little Rock Scripture Study and St. Peregrine's Angel Network.

Maybe the question should be where do we start? Remember, you're not alone. God will eventually put you where He needs you. Begin with prayer and the Sacraments of Reconciliation and the Eucharist. Ask Him to forgive your past sins, such as ignoring the calls, so that life will begin anew, free of those encumbrances.

Father Al once wrote, "Because our true identity is based on our relationship with Jesus, we don't know ourselves if we don't know Jesus. If we don't know Jesus and ourselves, we have very little idea of what life is all about."

Reintroduce yourself to Christ. Remember, Jesus celebrated the first Mass, the last supper, not on a Sunday, so make this introduction at a weekday Mass. It will show God you are serious, and you will be surrounded by a community of believers all working on conversion. From this point, center your life on the Mass and the Eucharist. The Mass is far from boring, once you truly participate. It will become more and more exciting each time, as you start to feel His presence. You will want to become an integral part of this faith community, plus you will see some of the ministries in action..

Now, jump in with both feet, get involved. If you feel a need for greater knowledge, try one of the instructional groups like RCIA (Rite of Christian Initiation for Adults). Remember, it's not just for non-Catholics. Of course, there is always my favorite – Bible Study. Almost every parish we visit has one, although sometime they are grass roots groups, not an official ministry As long as the material is Catholic, you're on your way.

As we pray for discernment, the destination may not immediately be made clear. Like the old radio show, The Shadow, the evil spirit and even our own spirit can cloud men's and women's minds' so we will not hear His word. Persevere.

Over the years, Valerie and I have experimented or considered numerous stewardship opportunities, but often did not feel called, gifted or even comfortable

Step 6 – Lifestyle

and so moved on. Eventually, being docile to the Holy Spirit, we all find our places in the Body of Christ. You will know by the almost euphoric and yet peaceful feeling of participation and belonging. Not only does it become a joy rather than a burden, you will begin to share that enthusiasm with others and truly enjoy the glory of being a Eucharistic minister, or the friendship of being a greeter. These are just typical rewards for becoming faithful stewards. I still tell everyone that I get more out of the Bible study than any of the participants. Give it a try. Get out of the secular rut. Quit building your own house and start helping to build the Kingdom of God, here in your very own parish.

If you still don't appreciate the blessings of Catholicism, let's look at another offering by Father Al from OBOB July 24, 2003:

Less than one-third of the people on earth have been baptized into the church and have become children of God. If you are in that number, consider yourself very blest.

> Less than one-fifth of the world has received Holy Communion – even once. A smaller percentage of these people have the opportunity of going to Mass weekly. Less than one percent of the world go to Mass and Holy Communion daily. If you have received Communion, if you can go to Mass without traveling for hours or days, how "blest are your eyes because they see

> and blest are your ears because they hear" (Matthew 13:6).
>
> If you have ever read part of the Bible, held the Bible in your hands or even own a Bible, you are a minority in the world. Hundreds of millions would love to trade places with you. Jesus declares: "I assure you, many a prophet and many a saint longed to see what you see but did not see it, to hear what you hear but did not hear it" (Matthew 13:17).
>
> I could go on, but I'll leave it to you to count your blessings further. It is safe to say that you are probably among the most blessed people in history. "When much has been given a man, much will be required of him. More will be asked of a man to whom more has been entrusted" (Luke 12:48).

Presentation Ministries, publisher of OBOB, offers a complete series of tapes and booklets on Catholic lifestyle, including everything from prayer and the sacraments to sex and money.

We don't have to be confused, frustrated, depressed, stressed or unhappy. Peace, happiness and fulfillment are as accessible to us as the decision to follow Jesus. In summary, allow me to offer a few lifestyle suggestions that worked for me:

Do first what's important to salvation – yours, your family's and all those God has given you. Participate in Mass and the Sacraments frequently. People spend hundreds of dollars to hear motivational speakers, but

Step 6 – Lifestyle

once you learn to love Jesus and His Mass, you will have all the encouragement available to humans and beyond. You will be touched by many homilies from those Spirit-filled priests and deacons. And, <u>don't leave early</u> – you will miss the blessing and the power to go spread the Good News to the world. Believe me, we need it. Be loyal to your parish but feel free, as we do, to attend Mass at surrounding churches and participate in the soul of other communities. Remember, we are all one Body.

Except for serious illness, we never miss Sunday Mass. At home, traveling, or camping, we schedule Mass first, and everything else can follow, not just because we are commanded to *keep holy the Sabbath*, but because of our love for the Liturgy of the Word and the Eucharist. Besides, life would be empty without the celebration. Frequent Mass is also a wonderful way to evangelize. Even our non-Catholic friends and family take note of our religious observances. Especially during the week, I tell people, "I'm going to church." It's not bragging, it's evangelizing.

Observe the Sabbath. Don't shop on Sunday. Make it a family day, with the Lord. In addition to the Mass, join in the other Spirit filled activity of your parish and the others around you. <u>Read the church bulletin</u> and subscribe to the diocesan newspaper to know what is being offered in the area. Seek especially those life-changing opportunities like retreats, missions, and workshops. Frequently place yourself and others in the near occasion of God's grace. And, of course, read, study and pray Scripture, always.

Remember, the Bible came from the Catholic church, not the other way around. Actually, the church existed for about 300 years before the cannon of Scripture was organized.

Enjoy <u>good</u> books and the limited number of movies and TV offerings appropriate for human consumption. Look to your local Catholic or other Christian stores for books, tapes and DVDs. Don't allow children or adults to partake of entertainment that is not suitable, even if "everyone else is seeing it." Be a parent, not a peer, to your children. Life is to purify, not gratify.

Celebrate your faith and holy days as you would special secular events and holidays. Have a family party to recall your baptism as well as your birthday. For all occasions give Christian gifts; the thought may last a lifetime. Give your love, always and to everyone, including yourself.

Do good works. Contrary to what many of the "feel-good churches" advocate, God does call us to do the works He has selected. Faith and good works grow together. To paraphrase a popular Christian hymn: "Let the rich help the poor, let the healthy help the sick, let the free help the imprisoned, let the moral help the immoral."

Which brings us to our role in the secular world. Get involved; be a voice in your community. Understand and support the Catholic position on important issues

Step 6 – Lifestyle

and encourage our church hierarchy to voice their position openly on secular offices and issues. Let us all make our stand known to the government leaders, especially to the so-called Christians in the political arena.

Use your blessings to glorify God. Everything is a gift from the Father, to be used for His purpose and returned when we are finished. Even after death we can continue our good works by willing everything He has given us back to organizations that will continue to use the resources to do His work. Praise God.

Allow Jesus to radically change your lifestyle, little by little. Growing in conversion, I lost interest in TV, the newspaper, movies, sports and other activities that are of no spiritual value. To understand the status of your journey, keep a journal. Record how God is acting in you life, and by all means, make special note of the God-Incidences that will become more and more frequent. My journal reveals growth in love and faith that often surprises even me. Regarding "God-Incidences," He may be calling me to compile a collection of these minor and sometimes major miracles. If so, I may be asking for yours.

Actually, the whole Bible teaches us how we are to live, but let me share just a few of the Scripture readings that have significantly impacted my life:

(Matthew 6:21): *For where your treasure is, there also your heart will be.* Examine your checkbook.

(John 14:12): *I say to you, whoever believes in me will do works that I do, and will do greater ones.*

(Luke 18:24): *How hard it is for those who have wealth to enter the kingdom of God.*

(Galatians 5:16-17): *Live by the spirit and you will certainly not gratify the desire of the flesh. For the flesh has desires against the spirit and the spirit against the flesh.*

(Philippians 2:14-15): *Do everything without grumbling or questioning, that you may be blameless and innocent, children of God without blemish in the midst of a crooked and perverse generation.*

(1 Timothy 6:10): *The love of money is the root of all evils.*

(James 4:17): *For one who knows the right thing to do and does not do it, it is a sin.*

(1 Peter 4:2): *Do not spend what remains of one's life in the flesh on human desires, but on the will of God.*

Now for your first Scripture reading assignment. Jesus, in His own words, provided great detail on how we are to live. Nowhere are His instructions clearer than in the following passages:

> Matthew, chapters 5, 6 and 7
> (The Sermon on the Mount)
> and
> Luke, chapter 6:20-49
> (The Sermon on the Plain)

Step 6 – Lifestyle

Once you have read, studied and meditated on these Words, you may say, "Everything I need to know about life, I learned from Jesus."

Long before He walked this earth, God gave us lifestyle direction. Joshua, after offering alternatives to the people of Israel, makes his own intentions perfectly clear, *"As for me and my household, we will serve the Lord"* (Johua.24:15).

The wisdom provided in "The Book of Sirach 3:17-23" elaborates on the lifestyle characteristic that is most difficult for people to grasp, especially for citizens of the United States: Humility.

*My son, conduct your affairs with humility,
and you will be loved more than a giver of gifts.
Humble yourself the more, the greater you are,
and you will find favor with God.
For great is the power of God:
by the humble he is glorified.
What is too sublime for you, seek not,
into things beyond your strength, search not.
What is committed to you, attend to:
for what is hidden is not your concern.
With what is too much for you, meddle not,
when shown things beyond human understanding.
Their own opinion has misled many,
and false reasoning unbalanced their judgment.*

There are three other areas of lifestyle that by sheer significance merit special mention. The first is spoken of so frequently by our non-Catholic brothers and sisters that it must trouble and possibly influence a number of our lukewarm Catholics. The issue is that faith alone is sufficient, without good works. Many go so far as to teach that all that is required for salvation is to say: "I accept Jesus Christ as my personal savior." First of all, we don't get to choose God. He chooses us, to follow wherever He leads. And He leads us through the Holy Spirit to do the good works that the Father has predetermined for us so as to fulfill our role in His grand salvation plan, and we best not ignore them. I could try to explain the few verses that talk about faith alone, but that is best left to the apologists, and I make no claim to that role. I will offer a few passages that are meaningful on the subject of lifestyle:

(Ephesians 2:10): *For we are his handiwork, created in Christ Jesus for the good works that God has prepared in advance, that we should live in them.*

(John 5:28-29): *All who are in the tombs will hear his voice and will come out, those who have done good deeds to the resurrection of life.*

(James 1:22): *Be doers of the word and not hearers only.*

And for your second Scripture reading assignment, try from "The Letter of James," chapter 2, verses 14-26. I rest my case.

The final two areas of lifestyle may be included here more for my benefit than yours, for I have struggled with them all of my adult life and continue even to this day, this moment. Yet they are mentioned more in the

Step 6 – Lifestyle

Word of God than most other virtues. Jesus instructs over and over and over about <u>love</u> and <u>the cross</u>.

Step 7 – Love

We all recognize love, because our Savior made it so clear. He even told us the two greatest commandments, above all others, are simply about love. *"You shall love the Lord, your God, with all your heart, with all your soul, and with all your mind. This is the greatest and the first commandment. The second is like it: You shall love your neighbor as yourself. The whole law and the prophets depend on these two commandments."* (Matthew 22:37-40)

We are called to love everyone, even our enemies. This, oddly enough, may be, for me, the least difficult, since I consider no one my enemy. So why the struggle? Possibly it stems from a lack of understanding. What does it mean to love? To love my wife is easy – there is a true feeling of warmth and joy and peace together. We can feel that. The same is probably also true for family members. We can feel that. But, what about God, whom we have never met or even talked to on the phone? How can we feel that? And what about everyone?

Step 7 – Love

To love God we must know God. It's that simple. I again submit that the best place to start knowing God is through His word, Scripture. In those words we learn how much God loves us: the Father gave his only Son, The Son; Jesus gave His life; and together they gave their love, the Holy Spirit. It is a natural instinct to return love, and so I learned to love God by realizing how much He loves me, loves us, everyone. The most recent revelation came when I finally began to feel His true presence in the Eucharist. Now with Jesus I feel warmth, joy and peace. With all my heart and all my soul and all my mind? It's coming.

Which brings us to everyone else. If God loves us all, even our enemies, how can we rationalize not loving everyone else? How can we justify doing anything less? Does that mean we are to feel warm and fuzzy about everyone in the whole world? For me, I don't think so. Probably my biggest stumbling block to love is selfishness of my things, my time and myself. A close second was lack of self-love. What does that mean?

The first significant change occurred when I read somewhere, "We can't love everyone, but we can be there for them." I could handle that idea, even though it meant sacrificing some of my selfishness.

Next came the understanding that negative feelings vanished when I prayed for an individual, and so I began to pray for those I most needed to love, starting with family. It worked. That, I now realize, is the same as

C.S. Lewis' description of Christian love as "wanting good for someone." Hopefully, in prayer for others we don't ask God for misfortune. Don't spend a lot of time asking God for lightning to strike the noisy neighbor – it's not going to happen. The idea of "wanting good" allowed me to understand self-love. Obviously, most of us want good for ourselves.

So now, with lots of prayer and loving grace from above, I can honestly say:

> I don't hate anyone.
> I love (want good for) everyone.
> I love (want good for) myself.

I am, however, still a work in progress regarding love, for I continue, on decreasing occasions, to guard my time, space and things, which probably keeps me from being there for everyone who needs me. The trouble with being self-centered is not recognizing when others really need. Become God centered.

There is another phrase that is key to loving, and yet I struggle with it daily. Whenever feeling selfish, unloving or uncaring, when your plans are interrupted by people with other plans, try these four words, "It's not about me." It's not about me, it's not about you. It's about your spouse, child, sister, brother, mother, father, friend, or even enemy, it's about the beggar, the homeless, the sick, the dying. Most of all: "It's about God." It's Not About me.

Step 7 – Love

Finally, most of us, probably all of us, want to be loved. It must be easier for someone to love a loving person. Maybe my friends, family and all should consider a prayer left for us by Father Al: "Father, may I love those considered unlovable."

Three final thoughts on love before we look at it in Scripture:

> 1. Again from Father Al, God is love, but not just any kind of love. He is "agape love," that is, unconditional love.

> 2. Expanding what C.S. Lewis says in Mere Christianity: "Charity means love in the Christian sense. But love, in the Christian sense, does not mean an emotion. It is a state, not of feelings but of will, that state of will which we have naturally about ourselves and must learn to have about others, that state of, 'wanting good.'"

> 3. From Father George Dunkley, probably the shortest and most understandable explanation of the Holy Trinity: The Father and the Son eternally, completely and perfectly love each other, and the manifestation of that love is the Holy Spirit.

Love in Scripture must be addressed more than any other of God's teachings. The following selection of favorites has led to a deeper understanding of what love means:

(Luke 6:27-28): *Love your enemies. Do good to those who hate you, bless those who curse you, pray for those who mistreat you.* Agape.

(John 3:16): *For God so loved the world that he gave his only son.* Agape.

(John 13:35): *This is how all will know you are my disciples, if you have love for one another.*

(Galatians 5:22): *The fruit of the Spirit is love.*

(1 John 4:8): *Whoever is without love does not know God, for God is love.*

Your third Scripture reading assignment is the best known dissertation on love, for wedding ceremonies, from "The First Letter of St. Paul to the Corinthians," chapter 13.

It may be of interest to end where we began about love: *"You shall love the Lord, your God, with all your heart, and with all your soul, and with all your strength.* Okay, which one? Matthew 22:37-39, Mark.12:30-31, or Luke 10:27-28? No, none of the above. This was written thousands of years earlier by Moses in "The Book of Deuteronomy," chapter 6, starting with verse 5 and continuing through verse 9 with: *Take to heart these words which I enjoin on you today. Drill them into your children. Speak of them at home or abroad, whether you are busy or at rest. Bind them at your wrist as a sign and let them be as a pendant on your*

Step 7 – Love

forehead. Write them on the doorposts of your houses and on your gates.

Step 8 – The Cross

Transition to the final topic of lifestyles was provided in about 597 BC by the prophet Ezekiel and amplified on March 14, 2003 by Father Al: *The Lord's way is not fair* (Ezekiel 18:25). It is beyond fair, it is the way of love and mercy, it is the way of the cross (Father Al).

During the wonderful era of the 50s, when I went from teen to young adult, except for newscasts, there was very little gloom and doom in books, film or other media. We could always look forward to a happy ending. Even in the serials, when it looked like the hero had been destroyed, there was always next week when we found what really happened and the good guy had actually survived. Maybe that sounds like a naive, Pollyanna lifestyle, but most of us from that time look back with true fondness. So it may not seem consistent for a child of the 50s to end this book of great hope with a subject so closely related to pain and suffering.

Step 8 – The Cross

Besides, the concept of the cross is so counter to today's culture.

Jesus says we must take up our cross daily. Advertising and other media forms try to convince us that no amount of suffering need be experienced in our lives, particularly here in the land of plenty, or should that be land of excess. True happiness is as near as a new car, house, dress, a can of beer or a new illicit sexual encounter. Anything less than real happiness can be rectified with just a little more money, unless you happen to be living in some slum or even worse, a third-world country. We have already noted that even many of our so-called Christian churches preach a feel-good doctrine that simply by accepting Jesus Christ as your personal savior, there is nothing more required. Maybe that's why you must go to a Catholic store to find a crucifix.

Until recently, for me the cross was very difficult to comprehend, probably because most of my life seemed to be lacking a real cross to carry. Oh, sure, we were a relatively poor family, but we always had food, clothing and a home, even if my oldest sister had to quit high school to work and help support us. And yes, our mother suffered most of her life in great physical and emotional pain, until she chose to end it. Would you expect less from someone with no education because her parents kept her working in fields and canneries? Our faithful and loving father died a few years later. They were both about 60. Both my sisters were, like me, alcoholics of varying degrees, both dead in their early 60s.

My first marriage, which as a cradle Catholic I believed would last forever, until death do us part, ended in divorce and annulment. Separated from my three children, my alcohol dependency grew, until it seriously affected my health, leading to heart disease. For 15 years life consisted of only work, brief family visits and drinking. Even later, with Valerie at my side, there were periods of struggle, in adjusting from lonely alcoholic to loving husband, father and grandfather.

And yet I never looked on any of these happenings as a cross, but maybe they were. For me it seemed like just a part of day-to-day living. But now, the closer I get to God, the more it becomes clear that, in each case, He was giving me the grace required to cope and grow on the way to conversion. Although it wasn't obvious at the time, with each pain there was an equal or greater outpouring of His love. Probably a better example would be the voluntary sacrifice, such as: giving up extensive RV travels so as not to interfere with the Bible study program or the cancer support group. It doesn't seem like much of a cross as compared to what Jesus carried for us.

We must also discern our suffering. Remember, the Father has allowed satan to reign in this world, so as citizens of the other world, the kingdom, we are going to encounter resistance. In some cases, like in "The Book of Job," God allows suffering as a test of our faith

Step 8 – The Cross

or for a far greater purpose. We can experience what may appear to be a cross by letting evil into our lives, but that is more of a self-created curse. With prayer and reconciliation God allows us to turn that curse in to a true cross when used for His purpose. My bout with alcoholism is an example through which God now permits me to help others struggling with addiction. But, alcohol was not so much a cross as a crutch.

A true God-given cross and more inspiring example is Valerie, a beautiful, vibrant woman, diagnosed with cancer the same year we were married, and only a few years after her husband had died of the same disease. Although healed through long periods of devastating chemotherapy and radiation, it left her body permanently scarred with the debilitating effects of fibramyalgia. It, however, did not scar her heart, mind or soul, and now through her own ministry, " St. Peregrine's Angels Network," there is hope and comfort provided to other cancer victims. This, I believe, is carrying the cross of Jesus for His purpose – love. It's up to us what we do with our cross, how we grow with our cross.

A cross can be a blessing for many if we simply follow the example of Jesus in saying, *Father, not my will but yours.* We are called to be like Jesus, who suffered unbelievable pain and suffering for the salvation for all that follow Him, all the way to Heaven. Being cured of all illness may not be a blessing; we can still go to hell in perfect health.

To paraphrase Father Benedict Groeschel: "The worst thing that ever happened, the crucifixion, is also the best thing that ever happened, salvation."

Pray, as St. Francis wrote: "We adore You O Christ and we praise You, because by Your holy cross You have redeemed the world." Also, according to Father Al: "Jesus, may I live the life You died on the cross for me to live."

Like love, the cross is mentioned frequently in Scripture. Of course there are the accounts of Jesus carrying the cross on the way to his crucifixion and our salvation, but also, in keeping with our theme, there are numerous passages exhorting us to take up our cross, even daily. For example:

(Matthew 10:38): *Whoever does not take up his cross and follow after me, is not worthy of me.*

(Matthew 16:24): The Conditions of Discipleship *Then Jesus said to his disciples, "Whoever wishes to come after me must deny himself, take up his cross and follow me."*

(Luke 9:23): *He must deny himself and take up his cross daily.*

(Luke 14:27): *Whoever does not carry his own cross and come after me cannot be my disciple.*

(1 Corinthians 1:18): *The message of the cross is foolishness to those who are perishing, but to us who are being saved it is the power of God.*

(Galatians 6:14): *But may I never boast except in the cross of our Lord Jesus Christ.*

Step 8 – The Cross

(Hebrews12:7): *Endure your trials as discipline, God treats you as sons.*

Lest we get overwhelmed by thoughts of suffering, remember, we do not carry the cross alone. Take heart in God's words in your final reading assignments: (Matthew 11:28-30 and 1 Corinthians 10:13). There is no greater joy for us humans than sharing in the carrying.

> Show your true belief – make "The Sign of the Cross" in public.

Step 9 – Conversion Revisited

Now, is that all there is???

For the book? Almost. Just a few more personal observations and the obligatory reference materials, included in the Appendix.

For conversion? Not even close, probably. Well, actually, we don't know how near or how far. Conversion is a lifelong journey, so only our Maker knows the time. Valerie and I have been hearing more and more homilies and other lectures emphasizing that we must all have a conversion experience. So why do only a small percentage encounter such a change in their lives? Certainly not because God doesn't offer, for He does to each and every one. Maybe it's because we are afraid.

It's relatively easy to be a "good Catholic." I believe the only real requirements are 52 Sunday Masses per year and an occasional Holy Day, plus an equal number of dollars in the basket. Then there is the once-a-year mandatory confession and participation in the

Step 9 – Conversion Revisited

Eucharist. I think, that's all there is? But that is not the Catholic that Jesus calls us to. His kind of Catholicism doesn't appear to be that easy.

Maybe it's the reason the majority of cradle Catholics never get past the very earliest and simplest understanding of the faith. Most are not particularly anxious to take up a cross every day or even take the time to understand what that means. And that's all too bad, because trying to be a great, good and holy Catholic is tremendously exciting and, would you believe, fun!!! The joy from seeing God active in your life and the lives of others is unsurpassed by any other feeling.

If you choose not to climb the conversion mountain, I can only say, again, you don't know what you're missing!!! Although I'm probably still very far from that peak, each plateau holds more ecstasy than anyone should expect in their whole lifetime. And, with each level we will look forward, with great anticipation, to the next higher level of our relationship with God Almighty.

Should you choose to begin the journey, it's as simple as saying:

Open my heart, Holy Spirit, to receive Your word and enlighten my mind to understand. Strengthen me, Holy Spirit, to follow wherever You lead.

It won't be long before you are ready to acknowledge His presence with our closing prayer:

> **I thank You, Holy Spirit, for Your word.**
> **Make it a living reality in my life,**
> **a constant guide at my side, a lamp**
> **for my feet and a light for my path.**
> **Let it mold my mind and shape my heart**
> **into the image of Christ, my Lord,**
> **and in conformity to Your holy will.**

Then you, too, will begin to experience "*what God has in store for those who love Him.*"

Appendix

<u>Aids to Conversion</u>

The Bible. Most Scripture quotes, *in italics* are from:

> The New American Bible
> World Publishing

Prayers and Mediations:

> Novena to the Holy Spirit
> Apostles of the Holy Spirit
>
> One Bread, One Body
> Presentation Ministries
>
> the Word among us
> Joseph Difato
>
> Devotions to the Holy Spirit
> Pauline Books & Media

Bible Study:

> Little Rock Scripture Study
> Little Rock, Arkansas
>
> Presentation Ministries

Bible Study Commentaries:

> The Liturgical Press

Bible Study Aids:

> What You Should Know About
> the Word of the Lord
> Liguori
>
> The Catholic Church and the Bible
> Ignatius Press
>
> Inside the Bible
> Ignatius Press
>
> The Bible Almanac
> Thomas Nelson
>
> Roget's Thesaurus of the Bible
> Harper Collins

Books (non fiction):

> Mere Christianity
> by C. S. Lewis
> Harper Collins

The Essential Catholic Handbook
Liguori

Encyclopedia of Catholicism
Harper Collins

Wake Up America
by Tom Campolo
Harper San Francisco

A wide selection of Catholic books and tapes is available from:

Presentation Ministries, Inc.
3230 McHenry
Cincinnati, Ohio 45211
www.PresentationMinistries.com

Apostolic Letters and other Vatican documents
Pauline Books and Media

Christian Travel Books:

Liguori Guide to Catholic USA
Liguori

Catholic Shrines and Places of Pilgrimage
in the United States
National Conference of Catholic Bishops

A Place for God
Image Books, Doubleday

A Guide to Monastic Guest Houses
Morehouse Publishing

Books (fiction):

> This Present Darkness
> by Frank Peretti
> Crossway Books

> Piercing the Darkness
> by Frank Peretti
> Crossway Books

Retreats and Workshops:

> Called & Gifted Workshop
> The Catherine of Siena Institute
> Colorado Springs, Colorado

> Presentation Ministries
> Cincinnati, Ohio

> Mission San Luis Rey
> Oceanside, California

> Southern California Renewal Communities
> (SCRC)
> Burbank, California

Inquiries:

> St. Peregrine's Angels Network (SPAN)
> A Christian women's cancer support group

3529 Cannon Road, Suite 2B-513
Oceanside, California 92056
e-mail: val4span@netzero.com

Questions, comments and God-incidences should be directed to the author at:

Byways to Heaven
3529 Cannon Road, Suite 2B-513
Oceanside, California 92056
e-mail: BywaysToHeaven@netzero.com